C000214421

GLASTONBURY: The Complete Story of the Festival

John Bailey

HALSGROVE

First published in Great Britain in 2013

Copyright © John Bailey 2013

All rights reserved. No part of this publication may be reproduced, stored in a retrieval system, or transmitted in any form or by any means without the prior permission of the copyright holder.

British Library Cataloguing-in-Publication Data
A CIP record for this title is available from the British Library

ISBN 978 0 85704 217 0

HALSGROVE

Halsgrove House,
Ryelands Business Park,
Bagley Road, Wellington, Somerset TA21 9PZ
Tel: 01823 653777   Fax: 01823 216796
email: sales@halsgrove.com

Part of the Halsgrove group of companies
Information on all Halsgrove titles is available at: www.halsgrove.com

Printed in China by Everbest Printing Co Ltd

Pages 3, 131, 136 Images copyright © Dod Morrison Photography - www.dodmorrison.com and are included with his kind permission; Pages 6, 9, 10 Images copyright © David White and are included with his kind permission; Pages 11, 12 Text copyright © Andrew Kerr and included with kind permission. *Intolerably Hip The Memoirs of Andrew Kerr* is available as a paperback £14.99; Pages 16, 34, 36-39 and back cover, Images and text page 37 copyright © Dave Trippas 'Daytripper' and are included with his kind permission; Page 18 Image courtesy of Gianmaria Rizzardi; Pages 22, 23 Images copyright © Ron Reid included with Ed Buller's kind permission and www.ukfestivals.co.uk; Page 26, 29 Text copyright © memories www.ukfestivals.co.uk; Page 30 Image copyright © www.nubianrecords.co.uk/www.bristolarchiverecords.com by kind permission of Mike Darby; Page 31 Text copyright © www.bristolarchiverecords.com/bands.html#blackroots by kind permission of Mike Darby; Pages 40, 43 Images and text copyright © Kevin Redpath and included with his kind permission; Pages 42, 43 Text copyright © Nick Davies, journalist and included with his kind permission; Pages 45, 47, 52- 55, 57 Images copyright © Giacomino Parkinson; Pages 48, 49 Image and text copyright © Chris-www.retro-madness.co.uk and included with his kind permission; Pages 59, 60, 63-65 Images copyright © Traveller Dave and are included with his kind permission. Comprehensive details of Traveller Dave's images can be found at www.travellerhomes.co.uk and are available in the books *Traveller Homes* and *Traveller Daze*; Pages 68, 69 Image and text copyright © Ray Brooks-www.raybrooks.co.uk; Pages 71-73 Image and text copyright © Ray Laidlaw, Lindisfarne, and included with his kind permission; Pages 67, 74, 76-81, 87, 96, Images copyright © Simon Marsh-www.webm8.co.uk and are included with his kind permission; Pages 82, 83 Image and text copyright © Jojo Denovan-www.curefans.com and included with kind permission of Jojo and David Sanchez; Pages 89, 90, 91 Images copyright © Louise May and included with her kind permission; Pages 93, 102, 109 Images copyright © Jeff Spicer/Alpha/Globe Photos Inc/www.Image Collect.com; Pages 94, 95, 104, 106, 111, 124, 126, 129, 130 Text copyright © glastonburyfestivals.co.uk; Pages 95, 98, 105, 107, 111, 113, 115-118, 122, 123, 125, 127, 129, 133, 134, Images copyright © Hal Stephenson-www.halvin.co.uk and are included with his kind permission; Pages 100, 103 Images copyright © Dave Charnley/Globelinkuk/Globe Photos Inc/www.imagecollect.com; Page 101 Image copyright © Judith Anderson/Fly On The Wall Media.com and included with kind permission of Anthony Scott Piatt; Page 108 Steve Harley image copyright © Mike Callow and included with his kind permission; Page 112 Text supplied courtesy and copyright © Piney Gir-www.pineygir.com and *Guardian* report copyright © Jude Rogers. Image courtesy of and copyright © Ian Kellett/Piney Gir; Page 113 and front cover copyright © Mark Bracey - www.halvin.co.uk and are included with his kind permission; Page 119 copyright © JimDyson/www.istock.com; Pages 120, 121 Text and images copyright © www.Strummerville.com and included with kind permission from Jamie, www.strummerville.com and www glastonburyfestivals.co.uk; Pages 132, 135, 140 festival review copyright © www.virtual festivals.com and included with the kind permission of Chris Swindells; Page 137 Text copyright ©*The History of Skinhead Reggae 1968-1972*, John Bailey; Page 138, 141 Images copyright ©Jason Bryant www.glastonburyfestivals.co.uk and included with his kind permission.

Contents

Acknowledgements

I would like to express my sincere appreciation to Michael Eavis for the Foreword, and help editing the book, ensuring an accurate first hand history of the festival. Having spent time with Michael it is clear that his enthusiasm for what has been achieved is unwavering and some of the anecdotes revealed are a delight to have included. On my visits to Worthy Farm it is clear that this is a working farm transformed during mid-summer for an event covering just a few days, one that has earned the right to have established itself as a worldwide phenomenon. Michael introduced me to Andrew Kerr who so kindly gave permission to include part of his memoirs to ensure the early days, when the festival was conceived, are accurately documented; Michael also introduced me to Jason Bryant, and his stunning festival images.

Perhaps the most difficult part has been trying to discover early images of the festival. Remember if you can in 1970 there was no digital photography, and to own a good camera was not an affordable option for most. However, some came to light, and although the early images may not be as detailed as would be expected today, they evoke the true meaning of the early festivals. Many photographers have kindly given permission to include their work in the book, with my appreciation to David White, David Trippas 'Daytripper' who was one of the original hippies involved from the outset, and Traveller Dave, who himself has written a couple of books. My grateful appreciation goes to Hal Stephenson for his most generous contribution to the book, and Simon Marsh, both having provided a plethora of excellent images from the festival; their websites merit a visit. I would like to thank Ed Buller for arranging the excellent early images of Tim Blake, taken by the late great Aussie photographer, Ron Reid, and for Tim's kind permission to include them. Dod Morrison has also generously given permission to use some of his close-up photography in the book. Dod is a professional photographer who lives in Aberdeen. His photography has been published in *Big Cheese, Vive le Rock* and *Rock 'n Reel*, his work featuring on several CD's and tour posters. I would also acknowledge Reverend Barker for the permission to use comments from the excellent web site www.ukrockfestivals.com and Chris Swindells from www.virtualfestivals.com for his generous contributions. The list goes on, including Nick Davis, journalist, and Kevin Redpath, film and multi-media producer, writer and presenter; also Len & Molly Johns for their proof reading. As before I have to thank Tina for all her help and would like to acknowledge Steven Pugsley and his colleagues at Halsgrove for their ever-present professionalism and everyone else who has contributed to *Glastonbury: the Complete Story of the Fesitval.*

Recommended reading:

Intolerably Hip - The Memoirs of Andrew Kerr

Recommended web sites:

www.glastonburyfestivals.co.uk
www.virtualfestivals.com
www.ukfestivals.co.uk
www.halvin.co.uk
www.webm8.co.uk
www.pineygir.com

www.dodmorrison.com
www.travellerhomes.co.uk
www.strummerville.com
www.curefans.com
www.nubianrecords.co.uk
www.raybrooks.co.uk

Foreword **by Michael Eavis**

Worthy Farm has been farmed by the Eavis family as a dairy farm for well over 100 years.

However, I wanted to go to sea and joined the Union Castle shipping company when I was just seventeen. Unfortunately my father died only two years later so I had to come back home to run the farm for my mother who was still finishing off the raising of her five children.

After a harrowing twenty years trying to make the farm work, which included a two year spell of working down the coal mine at Chilcompton, the Bath Blues festival appeared at the showground at Shepton. Jean and I went there and enjoyed it so much that I was tempted to have a go myself. Jean thought I had gone crazy, but I did it the same year (1970) and I have never really regretted it.

There were doubts and fears, worries and sleepless nights but we got there in the end. Thankfully Jean grew to like it and she gave me the enormous support that I needed.

Forty-three years later the festival has now grown beyond my wildest dreams, it sells out 145,000 tickets in just over an hour and there are probably over half a million more people who would also like to come.

I wonder how much longer the Glastonbury ticket will remain so magical?

June 2013

The Beginning

The first festival was held over two days in the late summer of 1970, ironically the day after Jimi Hendrix died. Michael Eavis had been inspired by a music festival held at the nearby Bath & West Showground earlier that year, with an estimated 150,000 in attendance, all there to witness acts like Led Zeppelin and Pink Floyd performing from a large central stage. More significantly technology had

Setting Light To The Hay Cart: © David White. David said "It was about six in the morning and a bit chilly so a group of Hells Angels made the fire to keep warm."

arrived, allowing the images to be projected onto large screens; perhaps for the first time close up images of the acts were there for all to see. Whether or not true it has been suggested that Michael Eavis managed to get in through a hedge to witness the musical spectacular, a follow up from a festival held in Bath the previous year that attracted in the region of 12,000 people. The vision was conceived to hold a small festival of his own in the heart of the beautiful Somerset countryside on land at Worthy Farm, Pilton.

Two significant events had taken place in 1969, one across the pond in America where an estimated 400,000 revellers descended on a farm in Woodstock for a weekend festival. Perhaps more relevant and closer to home, the Isle of Wight Festival witnessed 500,000 taking part, events that were the embryo of the now traditional outdoor festival.

1970

The objective of the first Pilton Pop Blues and Folk Festival was to attract 1500 to the site with admission £1, but including the allure of free camping for the weekend and free milk from the farm. The line up showed that the festival had ambition, with The Kinks set to headline the event. The music was a foremost love but that first festival was geared up to provide funds to repay the farm's overdraft. As events turned out, the festival showed a substantial loss of £1500, a fate incidentally shared by both Woodstock and The Isle of Wight Festivals. With new laws quickly passed it was seen that the days of such great gatherings would be numbered. The first festival was sparsely attended, but it got the go ahead, despite opposition from the local authority and in particular, the police.

The festival at the time was described by some as badly advertised and poorly organised, not perhaps the best start, but nevertheless a precedent had been set for what would become one of the longest-running festivals.

The headline acts advertised were The Kinks and Wayne Fontana and The Mindbenders, but were replaced by Tyrannosaurus Rex, later finding international fame as Marc Bolan & T.Rex. The other acts on the bill included Stackridge, Quintessence, Ian Anderson and Al Stewart and other local bands including Marsupilami.

That the festival made a loss was no doubt assisted by the Hells Angels whom Michael Eavis had hired for security, getting drunk, and setting light to his hay wagon.

Pop Festival Held at Glastonbury

The line up for the inaugural festival included local folk group Stackridge, local band Marsupilami who opened the show and Marc Bolan, a last minute replacement for The Kinks, who arrived in style. Michael described to me his first meeting with Marc. *"His velvet covered car had to negotiate the overgrown and muddy lane to the farm and when I saw it I went to stroke it because it was covered in velvet and Marc Bolan screamed, don't touch my car man!"*

That evening Marc Bolan closed the show giving a performance that has ranked amongst the very best with the crowd transfixed as they played on a balmy summer's night. The atmosphere was dreamlike; with the sun setting behind the stage the seeds of the celebrated Festival were now well and truly sown. That year T. Rex made the transition from acoustic to a more electric sound with the release of *Ride A White Swan* said to have been inspired by Mungo Jerry's *In The Summer Time*. The single, released in July, sold at a snail's pace, finally entering the charts in October. Popularity gradually increased and it peaked at number two in January 1971, only eclipsed by the massive selling hit *Granddad* by the late Clive Dunn. The record earned instant stardom with a follow up *Hot Love* reaching the top of the pile where it remained for six weeks in the spring of 1971. In 1971 Bolan's record company Fly issued *Jeepster* without his permission, an act that saw him part company to join EMI who gave him his own label, The T. Rex Wax Company. Despite the unauthorised release the record made it to number two. Two more number ones followed in 1972 with *Telegram Sam* and *Metal Guru*.

Back in 1969 a disparate band of young musicians found common ground in the Bristol/Bath musical stew and gathered together in a group called 'Stackridge Lemon'. With a constant flow of changing line-ups, finally by late 1970 'Stackridge' (having dropped the 'Lemon') were Mike Tobin, Andy Davis, James Warren, Mutter Slater, Crun Walters, Mike Evans and Billy Sparkle. Already their somewhat eccentric mix of witty, often poignant lyrics, memorable melodies, extended instrumental passages and self effacing stage presentation was catching the attention of the music press and the live gig circuit.

"Marc Bolan was Extraordinary"

The Kinks backed out after the *Melody Maker* carried a story with the headline *'Kinks for Mini Festival'*. *"I think they were a bit insulted by that,"* Eavis says jovially. *"After all, they were at the top of the charts with 'Lola' at the time".* When they pulled out, Eavis, floundering, called their manager again and he said, *"Well, Marc Bolan's going past on his way to play Butlins in Minehead. He'll do it for the same money."* *"So I said, Fantastic – I mean, T. Rex was just really taking off then. All the posters still said it was The Kinks playing, though."*

It was very much a one-man operation that first year; Eavis collected all the money himself, as well as organising the stage and dealing with the musicians. *"Marc Bolan arrived in what I think was a Thunderbird,"* he says, *"a big wide car trying to make it down this narrow track, and he probably got a few scratches from the hedge, so he was quite grumpy when he turned up. Still, he recovered enough to play, and that performance remains one of my favourite memories of the past 40 years: It was extraordinary, and with that set I thought, if I can produce this, the festival's got a future."*

Opposite: *Scenes from the inaugural festival in 1970.*

Notable events from 1970

January
- The first Boeing 747 Jumbo Jet landed at Heathrow.

March
- Martin Peters became the first £200,000 footballer when he was transferred from West Ham United to Tottenham.
- Teenagers vote for the first time in Britain at a by-election at nearby Bridgwater, and would do so nationally in June at the General Election.

April
- Paul McCartney announced that he and the Beatles have parted company; the group would break up before the end of the year.
- Everton win the Football League First Division (as it was then) and Chelsea lift the FA Cup.
- The Apollo 13 mission to the Moon is aborted when an oxygen tank explodes forcing the mission to return to earth, but the space craft had to continue circumnavigating the Moon to ensure its trajectory would return them safely to earth.

May
- The world cup kicked off in Mexico with England's expectations high following their triumph on the hallowed turf at Wembley in '66.

June
- England go out at the quarter-final stage 2-3 to West Germany, conceding a two goal lead.
- Edward Heath's Conservative party are triumphant in the General Election.

October
- Oil was discovered in the North Sea.
- The Ten Shilling (Ten Bob) note was no longer legal tender.

This first festival was not a charitable affair although from 1979 onward that is the case. The aim of the first festival was to repay an overdraft. That was the plan but the festival lost money, and Marc Bolan left without his £500 fee but was happy to receive it in £100 monthly instalments, which were duly honoured.

The reaction from the crowd was somewhat mixed with some expressing how they enjoyed the serene nature of the surroundings whilst others found it too tranquil. Michael returned to the everyday life of a dairy farmer and to some extent that was it, or it was until Andrew Kerr stepped in, so onward to 1971.

Andrew Kerr remembers the 1971 festival...

During the summer of 1970 I watched the Isle of Wight Festival with some friends high above the site on a hill next to it, outside the fenced arena. Returning to London with a car load of friends I said "We've got to have a proper festival, one that has some cosmic significance. Let's do it at Stonehenge at the summer solstice!"

I visited Stonehenge and from what I knew about the stones they must have been there for reasons of celebration. Having been brought up on a farm I realised that as the land around the stones had acres of corn crops at Midsummer that would be half-grown and unripe. It was obviously very unsuitable to hold a large gathering especially if most of the crowd would come from the cities untrained in country ways. Drug crazed hippies charging around in the crops would not go down too well with the local farmers. So what about another sacred site such as Glastonbury?

During my search for a site to replace Stonehenge I received a couple of calls from different people telling me about a farmer in Somerset near Glastonbury, who had put on a weekend festival in his fields. One of them was Susan Malleson, next to whom we had camped at the Bath Blues Festival. Another came from Dave Trippas, the last of his line, he said.

I heard Jeff Dexter announce at a gig in Hyde Park that a festival was going to be held in Somerset the following weekend. It so happened that Jimi Hendrix actually died the night before the festival began.

Andrew Kerr.

Although I did not go to the Pilton Pop Festival as it was known locally, in September 1970, I telephoned the farmer who had staged it and we arranged to meet. I very much regret missing Marc Bolan and T. Rex.

On the evening before the appointed day, I drove down to Glastonbury and spent much of the sleepless night on the Tor with half a dozen friends. There I met Bill Harkin, who had a small blue van in which he had a supply of 'Gourmet Foods', which was painted on the side of it. "Would you like an oatcake?" he said. I accepted and he became a valuable member of the team. In the morning I went to Pilton to have a look at the site. There is a string of power lines on pylons crossing it and I thought, "No, it's no good, they are defacing the beautiful Vale of Avalon". Within me a little voice said "Ignore them and they will go away".

The site was a perfect amphitheatre with the Glastonbury Tor, seven miles away, commanding the valley. Later in the day I went to Hazel Mount, a small house in Pilton village. The meeting with Michael was a seminal moment.

I told him of my wish to stage a festival on his farm, which was to be free: a giving event which sought a spiritual awakening and a demonstration against greed. To my surprise he said, "Yes!"

By this time my hair was worn long and I had a modest beard. He had a little hair on his head but it was supported by the 'Newgate Fringe' of a beard so often seen in the rural West Country. He had a broad smile and a beaming face. What I was asking, even to me, seemed a bit loopy, and for the life of me I cannot imagine why he said "Yes". Anyway he did, and bless him for it. He was in love with his future wife Jean and he was feeling very romantic.

Although I sort of 'dropped out' I never really thought of myself as a 'hippy', but an unconventional attitude, the hair and beard seemed to suggest it. Yet Michael for years referred to me as a rich hippy, until he learned better. I have never been rich in my life and I am not certainly likely to be so. A dictionary definition of a 'hippie' (or hippy) gives the following:

'A person of unconventional appearance, typically with long hair, jeans, beads, etc, often associated with hallucinogenic drugs and a rejection of conventional values'. I was like that so perhaps it was true.

On 6 October I moved into Worthy Farmhouse, Michael was living in Jean's house in Glastonbury at the time. As I came through the gate and saw the house, a rainbow was spread across the sky above it. Was that a load of hippy nonsense?! It felt like an omen to me.

As soon as I moved into the house I was joined by friends eager to help. Mark Irons had been a hitchhiker I had previously given a lift to. Jytte Klamer arrived and Bill Harkin came from time to time with his gourmet contribution from his van, eventually moving in as the site architect. The most notable was Arabella Churchill a relation of the late Sir Winston Churchill. In 1971 she moved in and became a major force in the preparation for the festival.

 As the summer solstice of 1971 fast approached the scaffolding for the building of the Pyramid was ordered. Bill Harkin had told me when we first met that he had a couple of powerful dreams about the design for a pyramid shaped stage. I had immediately accepted the idea and I was well acquainted with John Mitchell's writings on pyramids and with whom I had discussed sacred buildings. The first scaffolding arrived on the 4 June so we had a party that evening. The scaffolding forming the shape of the pyramid was clad on the two sides and front with 'expanded' metal sheeting. In daylight it looked very scruffy but sparkled like a jewel at night when lit up by film lighting.

One of the important helpers and regular visitors was Nik Turner of Hawkwind, the band so named on account of the shape of his beak-like nose and his flatulent gifts. The local band Marsupilami agreed to play again as they had done previously opening the 1970 festival. They were an early progressive rock band that migrated to Holland.

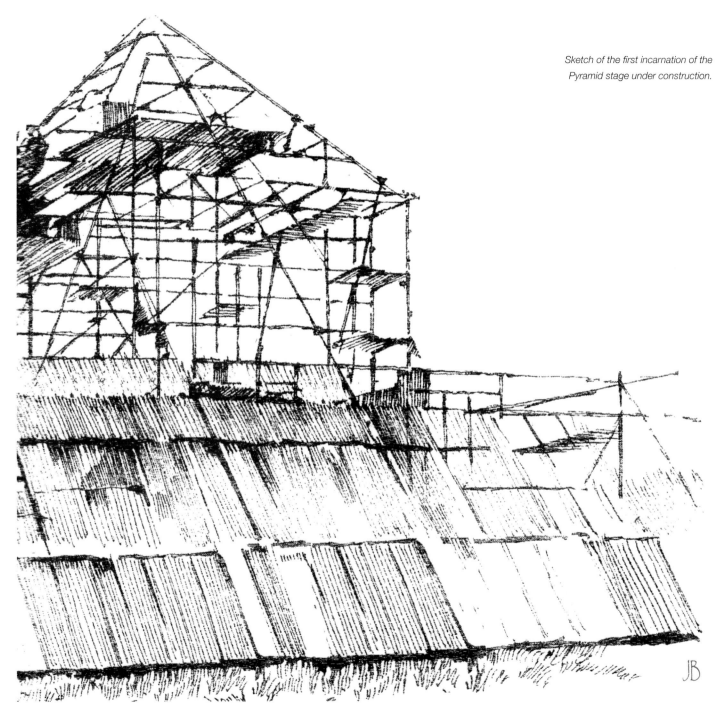

JB

1971

The Glastonbury Fayre

22 – 26 June

The second festival held at Pilton in 1971 was in reality The Glastonbury Fayre. The fayre was the brainchild of Andrew Kerr and featured the first incarnation of the Pyramid stage with admission free. The date had changed to coincide with the summer solstice. 12,000 people turned up to the three-day event headlined by David Bowie but not everyone was excited. Several local residents complained of the congestion and the noise as the music continued through the night. Even Michael Eavis was said to be concerned about the effect of the noise on his livestock and vowed to put an end to the fayre.

As the memories of the 1970 festival were fading and the dairy farm was returning to a rural tranquillity Andrew Kerr paid a visit to Michael Eavis with the idea of running a free festival at the farm the following year. The 1970 Isle of Wight Festival, following on from Woodstock the previous year, was attended by an estimated 500,000 and with Andrew Kerr and his associates willing to help fund the event Michael Eavis saw this as a way to recoup the losses of the inaugural 1970 festival.

The funding came from Michael and Arabella Churchill, his friend, who had left London for rural Somerset to avoid the media. Arabella Churchill, granddaughter of the late Sir Winston Churchill was selected to attend a NATO conference as its ambassador but she refused to go, citing her beliefs in the peace movement and was said to have been horrified at the events in 'Vietnam'.

Despite Michael's doubts, the eco warriors of their day were determined to see the festival through to completion with the five days of music, dance, and theatre of 1971 being remembered as a significant turning point in the history of green awareness.

Glastonbury Fair Manifesto, 1971

Glastonbury Fair will be held at Worthy Farm, Pilton, near Shepton Mallet, Somerset, from Sunday 20 June to Thursday 24 June, encompassing Midsummer's Day. It will be a fair in the medieval tradition, embodying the legends of the area, with music, dance, poetry, theatre, lights and the opportunity for spontaneous entertainments. There will be no monetary profit – it will be free. Man is fast ruining his environment, he is suffering from the effects of pollution; from the neurosis brought about by a basically urban industrial society; from a lack of spirituality in his life; and a spiritual awakening.

Glastonbury is rich in legends. It was here Joseph of Arimathea is said to have brought his young nephew, Jesus, and later to have returned with sacred relics to found the early Christian church in Britain. It was here that King Arthur and the Knights of the Round Table are said to have carried out their quest for the Holy Grail. It was here that the ancient druids are said to have been initiated into the secrets of the Universe and here the Priestess of Avalon kept the mysteries of the Earth. It is a magical place.

Worthy Farm lies in the Vale of Avalon some seven miles from Glastonbury. Pilton was once a port (although it is now 20 miles from the sea). Legend says that St Joseph of Arimathea and his nephew Jesus once visited the village on their way to the tin and lead mines nearby. The farm is 110 acres of pastureland forming a natural amphitheatre facing the proposed site for the stage. Glastonbury Tor stands at the edge of the valley and is clearly visible from all parts of the farm. The ley line between Glastonbury and Stonehenge runs a few yards from the stage site. The hills on the opposite side of the valley go to make up the sign of Sagittarius in the zodiacal plan; the country which lies between the farm and Glastonbury is Capricornus, and the Tor itself is Aquarius. The site lies on the solstice axis of the Zodiac.

The first Pyramid stage was constructed by Bill Harkin and his crew in 1971 out of scaffolding, expanded metal and plastic sheeting. The structure was built close to the Glastonbury Abbey/Stonehenge ley line and over the site of a blind spring.

Many believe that the pyramid shape is a very powerful structure, the apex of which draws energy up and transmits it still further while the energy from the stars and sun are attracted to it and drawn down. Those that saw the original Pyramid at night likened it to a diamond transmitting almost tangible energy as people danced on the stage.

The musicians who performed recorded a very rare album and the festival was captured on film by Nick Roeg and David Putman and released under the title 'Glastonbury Fayre'.

The impressive line up in 1971 in addition to David Bowie included Arthur Brown, Fairport Convention, Hawkwind, Joan Baez, Melanie, The Edgar Broughton Band, Family, and Pink Fairies.

Pink Floyd had undertaken a tour of Europe with the last date on the 20 June in Rome ahead of returning to England and Worthy Farm but their equipment was delayed and they were unable to perform.

The summer solstice festival was heralded by Melanie who in 1971 released the up-tempo, described at the time as whimsical, *Brand New Key*. The record soon became a huge international hit, topping the charts in many countries and reaching number four in the UK. Despite the record's provenance some had reported that the lyrics contained innuendo to the extent that some radio stations banned the record. Melanie was reported at the time to have said that she wrote the song in fifteen minutes as a cute thirties tune with the lock and key being Freudian symbols.

David Bowie's performance was set for the 22nd but the timings were way off course and he eventually performed his set on the 23rd at dawn. He was scheduled to play solo, but harmonies were provided courtesy of an impromptu appearance from a Scandinavian lady, who briefly joined him on stage, much to Bowie's amusement.

1978

The 1978 festival became known as the 'impromptu' festival. After persuasive discussion, a free mini festival did take place. There was little organisation and few facilities but somehow it did not matter. The stage was powered by an electric generator in a caravan with the cable running to the stage. The attendance was estimated at a mere 500.

The loss making festivals of 1970 and 1971 prompted Michael Eavis to rethink his strategy and abandon the inspiration, citing amongst other things too many hippies and too many drugs.

The rolling Somerset countryside with its close proximity to Stonehenge and Avebury continued to be a magnet for the hippies, sometimes causing conflict between their lifestyle, local residents and the authorities, but nothing on the scale that would be witnessed during the '80s. Towards the end of the decade in 1977, at Butleigh Wood a few miles west, close to Glastonbury, a convoy of free spirited souls arrived in July, estimated to be some three thousand who set up camp on a ridge above the woods, and with makeshift sound equipment they were able to celebrate seven o'clock on the seventh day of the seventh month in the year '77, presumably at 7pm not am.

The free festival was again scheduled at the same site for 1978 but as the police had blocked all access to the woods, the convoy stopped in their tracks. The police were now faced with a problem, they had prevented the festival at Butleigh Woods, but they now found themselves with a seemingly endless procession of vehicles that had nowhere to go; they had to go somewhere! The solution was to lead the convoy to Worthy Farm where Michael Eavis reluctantly agreed to take them, in with Nik Turner erecting a makeshift pyramid stage. The convoy were due to be there just for the one night but ended up encamped for three weeks, not an official festival but none the less a very significant event.

"The free festival at the farm in 1978 happened when a convoy had left Stonehenge after the solstice to go to another free festival we were planning. It was the early days of making the vision of festivals being a summer-long nomadic culture real. We'd identified a field at Cinnamon Lane in Glastonbury as the site, there had been a small alternative culture settlement there for a number of years, caravans and a tipi. I'd lived there myself. But when we turned up the farmers and police knew about it and had blocked off the access. The police radioed around and eventually came up with the venue of Worthy Farm, so we all headed there under police direction. I remember seeing Andrew Kerr there, and him saying this is better than '71."

NT

Opposite: *Neat wheels.*

1979

21 – 23 June

Now a three-day event and still referred to as the Glastonbury Fayre but with the theme of 'the year of the child'. Bill Harkin and Arabella Churchill were the instigators on this occasion and turned to Michael Eavis for financial backing. He secured a bank loan against the deeds of the farm. Special provision and entertainment was provided for children and it was at this event that the concept of the Children's World charity was born which still exists today and works in special schools throughout Somerset and Avon. Despite a crowd of 12,000, all paying £5 for entry, the organisers suffered a huge financial loss and no one wanted to risk another festival in 1980. It was also this summer that Michael's youngest daughter, Emily was born. Although the event made a loss, money was still found for the charities.

The 12,000 crowd enjoyed the likes of Peter Gabriel, Steve Hillage, Alex Harvey Band, Sky and the Footsbarn Theatre.

"In those days it was possible to leave the festival site, go to church on Sunday morning, have a couple of pints with lunch and be back for the first band to come on."

Michael told me that *"John Martyn did it for him, he hit all the right notes."*

Tim Blake who had started his career as a solo artist under the name of Crystal Machine, which is noted for being the first live act to introduce the use of laser lighting in the entertainment world, made a largely unheralded appearance at the festival. Tim was a member of Hawkwind between 1979 and 1980, as he is again today. He made his Glastonbury debut appearing after Peter Gabriel.

Tim wrote;

"Ah that's life, Glastonbury '79, I was announced, came complete with laser show, was paid! Then came a meeting with Michael and all and Gail Colson."

Michael, "Tim we would really like you to play last, and finish the festival off with your lasers and all."

Me, (swelling up) "Oh of course."

Gail, "Ok Tim, you'll be playing after Peter."

End of meeting I say to Gail, "who did you say you're working for now?"

"Oh I manage Peter, Peter Gabriel."

I almost fainted! I spent the whole evening shitting myself."

No jam though, just The New Jerusalem Set with Jean-Phillipe Rykiel. Peter played with a quickly assembled group, Steve H on guitar, Phil Collins on drums etc, they rehearsed every afternoon of the Festival and played so well."

TICKETS ARE SOLD SUBJECT TO THE FOLLOWING CONDITIONS.

1) The organisers reserve the right to refuse admission (ticket money paid may be refunded to anyone refused admission)
2) Tickets will not be exchanged or money refunded (except as above)
3) The organisers reserve the right to alter any announced billing of bands or other events.
4) The organisers reserve the right to make changes, if necessary due to unavoidable circumstances, to any of the Fayre arrangements.

A few notes from the programme are detailed below:

On the site

This beautiful site is 150 acres and should be big enough for us all. There are lots of maps around and notices on our boundary fences. So please don't go into our neighbours' fields. Some of the fields have been re-seeded this year and will be ruined if walked upon; cattle will need every blade of grass they can find after the past very poor winter and spring. If you go wandering in the fields off the Fayre site our farming neighbours will be upset – justifiably – and may try to prevent future Fayres. So use your heads – please! We have provided lots of wood for you, so please don't use the trees or hedges for wood. Please use only the fire sites provided as we must avoid additional fire risks. When setting up camp please keep within the lines we have set out with baler twine. And leave sensible gaps between tents. There are lots of rubbish bins and bags around the site, please use them. We hope we have provided you with all the facilities you might need for the three days, and that you won't need to go off site to get things. Pilton is only a small village so again, use your heads!

And the less we disturb the village and locals, the more chance we have of being able to do something like this again. We have worked hard to make this event happen, and you have paid towards it. It is now yours. Care for it, participate in it and make it perfect. Have a beautiful time.

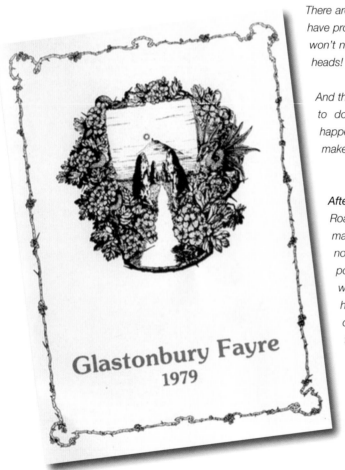

Glastonbury Fayre
1979

After the Fayre

Road: Petrol supplies are somewhat limited at the moment in the West Country, and many of the local garages have to close at weekends. Local supplies will certainly not be able to cope with the fuel needs of everyone at the Fayre. So please, if you possibly can re-fuel on your journey home, to leave enough fuel near here for those who really are short. Motorway service stations are always open, and we should have information on other garages closer to hand. Rail: The nearest station to London is Castle Cary with trains at 18.45 and 20.10 on Sunday. We hope to be able to run a coach service from the Fayre to meet these two trains. Trains from Bath go to London quicker and more often, at 4 minutes to and 6 minutes past the hour from 13.06 onwards. We will have information on trains for other places at the site information office.

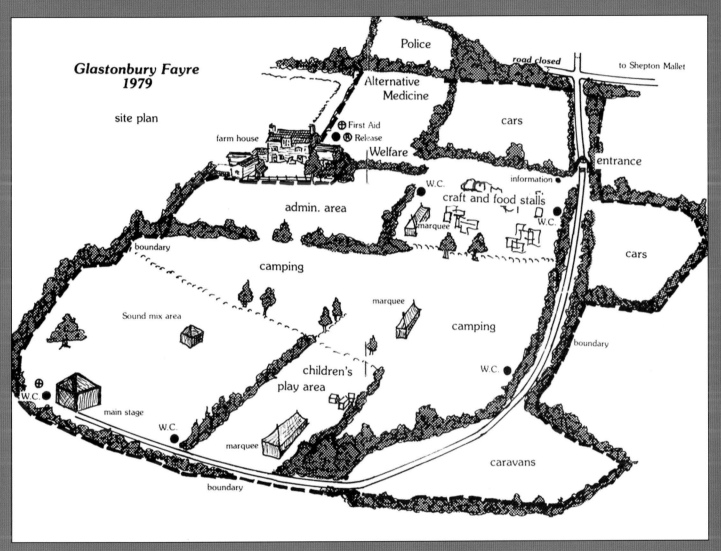

Glastonbury Fayre
1979

site plan

Police

road closed

to Shepton Mallet

Alternative
Medicine

cars

⊕ First Aid

● ® Release

farm house

Welfare

entrance

information ●

admin. area

W.C.

craft and food stalls

marquee

W.C.

boundary

cars

camping

marquee

Sound mix area

camping

boundary

children's
play area

W.C.

⊕

W.C.

main stage

W.C.

marquee

caravans

boundary

The site plan from 1979 covering a small area in comparison to the festival's present acreage.

Timothy 'Tim' Blake, is a keyboardist, synthesist, vocalist, and composer with both Gong, and Hawkwind. Tim is best known for his synthesizer and light performances as Crystal Machine, with the French light artist Patrice Warrene.

The outstanding images of Tim at Glastonbury Festival 1979 are courtesy of Ed Buller, a close friend of their Aussie photographer the late great Ron Reid.

1981

19 – 21 June

After the loss of 1979 there was no festival in 1980. Michael Eavis could not risk losing the farm and was determined to run the festival on a sound financial footing, to secure its long term future. This was made possible with an agreement with CND (Campaign For Nuclear Disarmament) that funds raised would benefit CND in return for them overseeing promotional material and ticket sales. 1981 also saw the second incarnation of the famous Pyramid stage, replacing the original temporary construction. The new construction doubled as a cow shed and animal food store during the winter months. This year the festival would need a licence from Mendip District Council and would have to overcome objections from local residents.

The 'Fayre' was replaced for the first time with 'Festival'. The original Glastonbury Festival, a slightly different affair, had run from 1914-1926. These festivals were founded as music events, Glastonbury chosen due to its strong Arthurian connections and ancient associations. The name change to Glastonbury Festival saw Michael Eavis at the helm, his responsibility to provide the money, arrange entertainment and organise the event, liaise with the authorities and organise market stalls etc. It took two months to build the permanent Pyramid stage out of telegraph poles and ex-MOD metal sheeting. Michael told me that, *"The CND logo from the stage was taken down by hippies who did not empathise with my political views. I went to get the cows in for milking around 5am and noticed it was no longer there, they had removed it from the stage area. It actually took me ten years to discover that it was in fact the hippies that I had employed at the festival who were responsible for removing it."* The CND logo was made of wood during carpentry classes at the nearby Evercreech village school. Michael Eavis eventually handed over approximately £20,000 to a very grateful CND.

Acts included: Aswad, Decline and Fall, Gong, Gordon Gilltrap, Ginger Baker, Hawkwind, John Cooper Clarke, Judy Tzuke, Matumbi, Nick Pickett, Robert Hunter, Roy Harper, Supercharge, Taj Mahal, Talisman, New Order, Rab Noakes, The Jazz Sluts, The Sound, Hinkleys Heroes, Beverley Martin, Chicken Shack and Pete Drummond.

A few thoughts from the programme:

> *Due to opposition from the local planning authority, there is a REAL possibility that this could be the LAST Festival to be held at Worthy Farm. Much depends upon the way in which this year's Festival is conducted. Each person present can make an important contribution by ensuring that NOTHING happens to spoil our good record, or give anyone cause to complain. Letters of support would be greatly appreciated sent to: Mr R Bush, Chief Planning Officer, Mendip District Council, Highfield House, Shepton Mallet, Somerset.*

> *We have worked hard to make this event happen, and you have paid towards it. It is now yours. Care for it, participate in it and make it perfect. Have a beautiful time.*

The Entertainment

The 1981 festival was more organised with additional stages, a theatre and a cinema. There was also a greater mix of bands with New Order playing their first gig. It was something of a surprise when New Order were booked to appear in the middle of a bill that featured such hardy Glastonbury perennials as Hawkwind and Roy Harper as the group had only recently reformed, a reincarnation of Joy Division due to the untimely death of singer Ian Curtis. The festival also included reggae with Aswad and Matumbi. As would be expected there were a number of speeches delivered from the stage concerning Nuclear Disarmament. Friday was possibly the best music night although Roy Harper's set was gate-crashed by Ginger Baker.

Roy Harper recalled;

"Later I'm playing the gig, going down quite well, building up to the finale. Then Ginger starts walking on with drums, setting up right in front of me, destroying everything. I couldn't believe it. So I left the microphone and said 'Hey, what you doing?' And he said, 'F—- off, you've been on here to f—-ing long, you c—-' and his band started bringing all their gear on. So I started to seethe, nudged one of his drums with my left foot and he lunged at me. I just burst, turned round and gave him one right in the guts. Ginger goes, 'Urrgghh you c——.' Then we were fighting and the stage was full of people. I completely flipped my lid."

"There we were at a festival dedicated to peace and love man and I hit someone. He may have been the thickest idiot at the festival but I'd actually hit him. After that I was filled with frantic remorse and basically just wanted to hit everyone, everything I could lay my bloody hands on. So they got hold of my arms and carried me off, looking like I'm ripe for Broadmoor, wearing this human straightjacket, screaming You f—-ing bastards. I'd lost it altogether; I was fighting f—-ing mad."

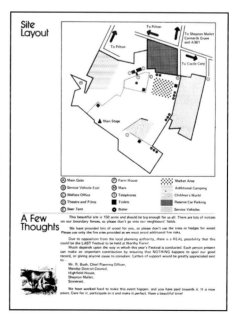

According to Harper the crowd then proceeded to bottle Ginger, one hitting him on the head, whereupon Ginger carried on playing. Another source says that Ginger threw a can at Harper and it hit him on the head.

Peter Brkusic confirmed to me:

"I heard the story from Ginger and he told me that he played the whole gig, and on his drum kit was blood everywhere from his wounded head. I think he was very proud about this."

1982

18 – 20 June

The 1982 festival was well organised and will be remembered for many things including Michael Eavis reportedly asking the firework organisers to point a £70 firework in the general direction of an anti CND plane flying over the site, in an attempt to chase it away. Michael explained *"Bruce Kent was speaking on the main stage on Sunday when a plane flew over trailing a banner that read, 'Kremlin Loves You', the noise drowning out the speaker so I asked the firework organisers to fire a rocket at it. I met the pilot in court at a later date when giving evidence and he was prosecuted and fined £400, a lot of money back then, for flying over a crowded area without a licence. He then pointed to me sitting a few feet away and said to the magistrates, 'he nearly blew me out of the sky with his rocket,' and the magistrates just laughed."*

This year's festival was of course remembered mostly for the MUD, with the highest rainfall for a single day in 45 years recorded on the Friday.

Getting to the festival had now become a major problem with the traffic unable to cope well with the local lanes although nothing could be done about that. Broken down cars were at the root of the problem on site and around the village. CND involvement was at the heart of the festival and it was this year that Western Region CND took control of the entrance gates and Mid Somerset CND took charge of all the information. A crowd of 25,000 paid to come and see amongst others: Richie Havens, Roy Harper, Van Morrison, Jackson Browne, Aswad, Judy Tzuke, Steel Pulse, John Cooper Clarke, Climax Blues Band, Thompson Twins, The Blues Band, Talisman and A Certain Ratio. U2 were billed but failed to play. The success of this year's festival despite the muddy conditions was the foundation of the triumphs that would follow.

Memories are made of this:

"This was my first ever event of this kind – I'd seen nothing like it and attended mainly because of my interest in CND at the time. It proved a life changing experience and generated an interest in the festival that has stayed with me all my life, even during the wilderness years when I didn't attend. I remember catching a shuttle bus from Bath after seeing the sun fail miserably to rise at Stonehenge on the solstice. Met up with a girl, with whom I spent a very enjoyable weekend and generally had the time of my life. Black Uhuru I remember specifically because people just streamed towards the stage as soon as the bass started pumping out. The Blues Band were great, particularly when drinking lethal local scrumpy, and the company of said young lady. The real buzz was for Van Morrison, and having not heard any of him I stayed for his set. I am ashamed to say I got bored and left early. I bitterly regretted that in later years and was really glad I could make up for it in 2005 when I finally got the chance to see him play a full set. Oddly enough I don't remember the bad weather, but I do remember the mud, with people slipping all over the place and a giant mud slide that others were enjoying in the Pyramid field."

*ukfestivals.co.uk

The festival had now taken on a completely new style as the promotional poster shows, with a wide-ranging variety of entertainment available.

The Theatre featured Alexei Sayle, David Rappaport, one of the best known dwarf actors in television and film, and Incubus, a walk about group, while the Cinema showcased the blockbuster movies, Doctor Strangelove, Airplane, China Syndrome and Secret Policeman's Ball.

The poster advertising the festival confirmed tickets available 'on the gate' £9 Fri - Sat - Sun, £8 Sat - Sun and £7 for Sunday. It carried a 'stop press' just confirmed to headline Friday night at Glastonbury 'Black Uhuru'.

INFORMATION

"UNTIL WE ACHIEVE NUCLEAR DISARM-AMENT WE ARE LIVING ON BORROWED TIME"
Paul Weller

Another Midsummer Glastonbury Festival is to be held in June this year at Worthy Farm three miles from Shepton Mallet Somerset The Festival site is situated in the legendary Vale of Avalon, overlooking Glastonbury Tor, and here,we will be presenting three days of Music, Theatre,Films,and much,much more.

Musicians and artists from both sides of the Atlantic will be performing continuously throughout the event.There is a special srea for the children, a large market,and plenty of space for camping and car-parking.

To ensure a more pleasant and comfortable stay with us, many improvements to the site are under way. These include new toilet facilities, a cabaret tent and a large area devoted to the Women's Peace Movement.

As with previous festivals the proceeds are being donated to the Campaign fro Nuclear Disarmament. 1983 is a very important year for the C.N.D. and the whole European Peace Movement, so we hope that you will pledge your support by joining us for a weekend of peace and merrymaking in this beautiful setting.

TICKETS

Three -day advance tickets are available by post at £12 each from CN.D. (Festival) 11 Goodwin Street, London,, N4 3HQ. Camping, Car-parking, V.A.T, and all On-site events are included in the ticket pricePlease. enclose am S.A.E. with your application. All cheques and postal-orders are to be made payable to: Glastonbury C.N.D. Festival. Children under the age of 14 are admitted free.

TRAVEL

Travel by rail and coach both to and from the festival site is being arranged.Full details of this service will be announced in later editions of this handbill and in the press.

INFOLINE

An up to the minute information service is now in operation. Ignore the rumors and get the facts by ringing 01-263-0977

HELP

A restricted budget and increased overheads neans that we need as much help as possible in promoting the festival.One of the most successful and effective methods is for sympathetic magazines and publications to donate bfree advertising space. just let us know the size and copy-date and we'll do the rest.

Our ads come ready to paste-up and on time, so if you think you can help please ring John Andrews on Bath 9012250 333289

STALLS

For full details,application form and price list, please write to: Glastonbury C.N.D. Festival, (Stalls), Worthy Farm, Pilton, Shepton Mallet, Somerset, BA4 4BY. Tel: Pilton (074989) 254 Please enclose a large S.A.E. with your application.

Information on the forthcoming 1983 festival was advertised well in advance with the introduction of the handbill.

OFFICIAL
PROGRAMME
17th, 18th and 19th of June 1983. Worthy Farm, Pilton, Shepton Mallet, Somerset.

Music, Theatre, Films, Travel. Children's World. Campaign Events. Women's Peace Alliance. Four Pages of Events Listings.

Price: 50p.

GLASTONBURY CND FESTIVAL 1983

1983

17 – 19 June

1983 called for a licence to be obtained for the event since the introduction of the Local Government Act became law, giving local authorities the power to regulate such events by stipulating the conditions. Mendip District Council issued a Public Entertainment Licence which set a crowd limit of 30,000 and went into considerable detail about access roads, water supply, hygiene and so on. It was also the first year that the festival had its own radio station, Radio Avalon. £45,000 was eventually raised for CND and local charities. Bands included: Curtis Mayfield, The Specials, Fun Boy Three, The Beat, UB40, Marillion, Melanie, A Certain Ratio, The Chieftains, Incantation, King Sunny Ade and Black Roots.

"After a couple of years as a punter at Glastonbury, I was asked to help out with the site electrics by Graham, who was the festival's electrician at the time. He had got the job the year before by fixing the pyramid generator when it went live, had to switch it off using a broom handle! There were only a couple of us doing the electrics for the whole site, plus another couple doing electrics for the market area. It's not like it is now, all nice blue plastic plugs, it was a railway carriage full of old reels of wire and ancient metal breaker boxes. Everything was joined together with connector blocks which we put inside plastic bags and taped up to keep the rain out; luckily it was a pretty hot year. Most of the generators, apart from the one for the Pyramid, were old site 'gennys' or borrowed from the local carnival club, so it was quite a challenge keeping everything going. Just before the Pyramid stage opened on the Friday, all the electrics went and I happened to be first on the scene. I quickly traced the fault and replaced a couple of fuses and got it going again, at which point I was told I wasn't to leave the stage area during performance time for the rest of the weekend, which suited me down to the ground, spent most of the time watching bands from the side of the stage.

I remember Marillion being on Friday and Melanie on the Saturday. During Melanie's set, the Hells Angels invaded the stage and as there was no security then, any crew on stage had to deal with it. They were actually no problem, each taking it in turns to give her a kiss before we escorted them off stage. Later that night I saw her sitting behind the Pyramid, in a circle of the Angels, strumming and singing late into the night for them. PeeWee who was running the festival bar had got in a few Angels as security. Alexis Korner was the compere for the weekend on the Pyramid and at the end of the festival on the Sunday night he got together with a few other musicians and played for the crew. Sadly he died not long after, but it's a memory I cherish. I was there for a couple of weeks before the festival started and the entire crew catering was done in Charlie's caravan with him and his daughters doing the cooking. They were brilliant, kept everyone happy and supplied tobacco and papers as well as brandy coffees. The lasers were brilliant as usual, LSD (light and sound design) did the Pyramid lighting and the legendary Tony Andrews (turbosound) did the PA. There was very little in the way of radios then so all the communications were via telephone cables laid through the hedges and fields and back to a cabin with a telephone exchange in it. It all worked pretty well most of the time but funny seeing the old type telephones dotted round the site. Anyway for me it was a brilliant festival and I've been working there ever since."

Pete Wilson

Reggae Hit the Town!

1983 was the year the festival adopted a distinctive ska/reggae feel. The Specials with their regenerated ska and the chart topping UB40 who had covered several of the singles from the golden age of reggae, their trademark sound being the number one hit, *Red, Red, Wine*, a cover of a skinhead reggae track from 1969 by Tony Tribe. Local band from Bristol, Black Roots, continued the reggae sound.

Black Roots were a powerful and potent force in the British reggae music scene throughout the eighties and left a legacy of no fewer than ten albums and more than eight singles before bowing out of the public eye in the mid-'90s. Hailing from the St Paul's area of Bristol, the original eight-member band were formed in 1979 and quickly gained a large following by touring almost non-stop around the country, playing their brand of 'militant pacifism' roots reggae in the nation's major colleges, universities and festivals. They attracted the attention of television with appearances on BBC2's *Neighbours*, BBC West, HTV West and Rockers Road-show and popular radio, where live studio sessions for Radio 1's *In Concert* (broadcast April 1982), John Peel, David 'Kid' Jensen and Peter Powell led to a BBC Radio 1 sessions LP. Their first releases were on the Nubian Records label and an EP containing *Bristol Rock, Tribal War, The Father* and *The System* preceded their first single, in 1981, *Chanting For Freedom*. Jon Futrell in *Black Echoes*, labelled them; *"Quite simply, Black Roots are the next great hope for reggae in this country."*

Their debut album, entitled simply *Black Roots* and released in 1983 on the Kick label, saw them make their mark immediately on the national music scene, with the leading black music paper *Black Echoes* declaring, *"a blinding debut album from the best of the new British reggae bands."* It was a highly acclaimed debut for the group which consisted of Delroy O'gilvie, Cordell Francis, Errol Brown, Jabulani Ngozi, Trevor Seivwright, Kondwani Ngozi, Derrick King and Carlton 'Roots' Smith. Six of the band were Jamaican-born, while Smith and Seivwright hailed from Bath and Newport respectively. The Ngozi brothers were Rastafarians, as was lead vocalist Delroy O'gilvie, who shared the front spot with Errol Brown. The group's first single on the Kick label, *Juvenile Delinquent*, was taken from the album and released in the same year, bubbling just under the national singles chart. They also completed some tour dates in Europe as support to UB40.

The late John Peel was quoted; *"If anyone tells you that there is no such thing as good British reggae, first tell them that they are a herbert and then listen to Black Roots."*

Black Roots.

1984

22 – 24 June

In January 1984 Michael Eavis successfully defended 5 prosecutions bought against him by Mendip District Council alleging contravention of the previous year's licence conditions. All five charges were dismissed after a daylong hearing at Shepton Mallet Magistrates Court. The local council then announced that the licence for 1984 would cost £2000. The licence numbers were set at 35,000 and for the first time specific car parking areas were designated with stewards employed to direct the traffic. Messages were also broadcast on the radio advising people not to turn up unless they had purchased a ticket in advance. 1984 also saw the start of the Green Fields, as a separate area within the festival.

The attendance was the designated 35,000. Tickets cost £13 and the programme price was 80 pence. A creditable £60,000 was raised for CND and other charities. In 1984 The Band were unable to turn up because Levon Helm had shot himself in the leg; Weather Report played the main stage; Elvis Costello headlined the last night for almost three hours; and The Smiths set was invaded.

The Smiths, a defining moment

The addition of The Smiths on the line-up caused a great deal of out-cry as many felt it wrong that a popular band should play at the Glastonbury Festival, and the stage crew, most of whom were hippy, didn't approve. Michael explained:

"I heard a lot of gossipy stuff about a new band called The Smiths so I went with Jean to the student union hall in Bristol to see them. I was mesmerised by their new sound and Morrissey's original style. So I booked them there and then through a friend of mine called Martin Elbourne who was for a while their booking agent. That was in October before the festival in '84.

When they turned up and played, we had no fences around the Pyramid stage, and I had no idea how crazy it was going to be. Morrissey beckoned people to come on stage and they simply ran up on the stage itself and surrounded the band. I was there too! The set couldn't possibly last long because we were jammed like sardines in and around the musicians. So after forty minutes it had to stop. This, as it turned out was a most significant moment in the festival's history. There was a huge amount of press interest and some of my stage crew didn't understand what was going on because they were part of the '70s hippy culture and did not like to see change – they even posted an offensive running order back stage calling them The Smits!

The music press gave us a field day, and we never realised how this was going to affect our future. We had now almost overnight become a fashionable place to be and we were gradually becoming icons of the youth culture of Britain.

I would say that somehow the arrival of The Smiths had moved our event on from traditional hippy ways to what it is now, and is one of the reasons why we're so popular with the majority of young people in the country."

The Green Field

The first Green Field had arrived, although rumours circulated that it was a pre-requisite of Morrissey's contract that he had somewhere nice and quiet to lie down, although it was never confirmed.

The Green Field was the concept of Liz Eliot, to create a sanctuary away from the main nucleus.

The programme noted:

'Here you will find a new way of living which are developing new ways of viewing the Earth. We believe in and practise the principle of caring for the Earth, and caring for others.'

Some of the of events featured;

Yoga workshop for women
Peace education workshop
Women in politics
Answering awkward questions about animal rights
Sacred dancing
Questioning lifestyles

A notice on the site requested:

'Please keep our big circle free from tents, it's our valuable green oasis which everyone can enjoy only if the grass is allowed to see the sky. Help to keep the site clean too, by picking up litter. Rubbish bags are available at the information station. Please defecate only in the places provided.'

The Green Field was a true oasis in a sea of pandemonium.

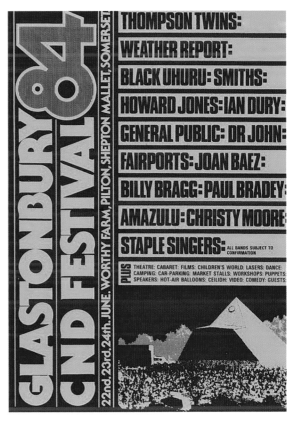

The line up on the flyer was as it stated subject to confirmation and the Staple Singers did not play and Elvis Costello headlined on the Sunday.

Memories are made of this

"Arriving at Glastonbury after Stonehenge, I got over the nonexistent fence and being a bit cream crackered, curled up on the high ground to the right of the farmhouse. A bloke had built a large cabin and had a settee next to a roaring fire, his detached luxury property was surrounded by a fence and he had a Union Jack up a flagpole. He watched as I pulled my coat over my head and crashed out in the warm sunshine.

Waking up next day about midday, the sun luckily had still got its hat on and hoping chummy with his acreage would give me a nice cuppa, "hi" says I, "do you know 69 people walked over you last night" says he and I didn't feel a thing. I wandered off for breakfast and soon met up with my friends and got into the swing of the festival."

Daytripper

Worthy Farm 1984.

I wished to forget who I was
and entertain the young hippies

Trying to write when so many were
hurting to love each other
yet the sea still lapped the shore
and the prime evil mud was not saying a word

I wanna be the guy with flowers and champagne
but I won't tell secrets
poverty is relative to the universe
but they'd heard it all before
paying money is not to heed the call

The video light winking at me warm
wishing it was childhood corn
and the sun locks that are never shorn
pass the blow here and suckle up to the milk tit.

The stars are glowing
and this life in my nail is a nit
grey coats and laser soft hair
free food kitchens
and a damp warm communal lair.

I'd forgotten who I was
listening to jazz
the suckling sea was roaring at me
dancing on a pinhead
talking to a tree.

Daytripper.

37

Everything stops for tea.
Opposite: *Alien at Glastonbury* and *Keeping Dry.*

"In my previous life as a professional photographer, I once shared a balloon ride with Michael Eavis who had commissioned me to take some aerial photographs of the festival fields after everyone had gone home to prove to Mendip District Council that he hadn't broken any planning guidelines. One warm summer evening in early July 1984, three of us set sail from Worthy Farm in a black balloon with the CND logo emblazoned in white on three sides. After drifting over the Mendips the pilot began looking for a place to land. We started to descend quite quickly onto what looked like a promising field. While the pilot managed the controls Michael and I looked over the edge of the basket and saw the rather alarming sight of the twin barrels of a twelve bore shotgun pointing directly up at us. An incensed farmer was screaming 'Don't you f***ing hippies dare try to bring that thing down in my cornfield.' Nothing focuses the mind more than being surrounded by four large propane cylinders, with only a tiny wicker basket, four hundred feet of gravity and a trigger happy landowner between you and your maker."

Kevin Redpath

1985

21 – 23 June

By 1985 Worthy Farm was considered too small to accommodate the festival so land from the neighbouring Cockmill Farm was purchased to enlarge the site by a further 100 acres. The weather was appalling and the site was drenched. The sheer size of the newly enlarged site meant that communications were stretched to the limit – the ultimate test for any organisation. Tractors were the only possible means of towing people off the site in the seriously bad weather. Michael Eavis was pleased that, *"we have had the mud bath and proved we can still cope with the conditions."* The site was steadily growing to the south, now crossing the old Somerset & Dorset branch line with the Green Field site relocated on the southern slopes, a site it retains to this day.

Tickets were priced at £16 with the programme steadily increasing toward a full pound at 90 pence. The attendance increased with the newly acquired land to reach 40,000 with £1,00,000 raised for CND and local charities. The acts this year included Roger Chapman, The Boomtown Rats, Echo And The Bunnymen, The Pogues, Ian Dury, Aswad, Hugh Masekela, Working Week, James, The Men They Couldn't Hang, Microdisney, Joe Cocker and The Style Council, and Michael Eavis' five year old daughter, Emily, who played violin on the Main Stage (followed by five encores).

Alexei Sayle addressed the audience *"a contact lens has been reported missing, can someone keep an eye out for it."*

By Sunday rain, rain and more rain had swamped the site, with the tractors having to provide a rescue service for the rain soaked, muddy campers who had simply had enough and upped and left. The torrential rain and the overwhelming mud made the headlines but they were eclipsed by events that had taken place a month earlier some forty miles away in Wiltshire during a beautiful summer's day, the weather being the least of the travellers' worries.

The Battle of the Bean Field took place over several hours during Saturday 1 June 1985, when the police prevented a convoy of several hundred new age travellers travelling from Savernake Forest to Stonehenge, the convoy made up of old buses and vans converted into living accommodation. The aim was to set up at the eleventh Stonehenge Free Festival in Wiltshire. The High Court had granted an exclusion zone of 4 miles around the perimeter of the stones to stop the event taking place. What followed was a notorious incident that was captured on film and reported widely amongst the media.

With the roads blocked the convoy became trapped, unable to continue their journey towards Stonehenge, and the police refused to allow them to return to Savernake with their vehicles. There were attempts by convoy members to negotiate with the police over several hours. The Chief Constable said that he was convinced that they were intent on breaking the exclusion zone that had been imposed around Stonehenge by the judiciary at the behest of English Heritage. There were outbreaks of violence in which several members of the convoy received head injuries. An ambulance was allowed through to take them to hospital. Eventually the police, some in riot gear entered on foot. Many attempted to escape in their vehicles, crossing over into the adjacent bean field; but the rough field terrain meant their vehicles were so slow that they were quickly overtaken by foot policemen. As a result, almost all of the members of the convoy were arrested.

The solstice gathering remained banned for many years and, as a consequence, Glastonbury Festival became a sort of Stonehenge as well as Glastonbury Festival. Michael Eavis was quoted as saying, *"I was seen as being very benevolent, but it was very difficult to manage and a lot of my staff left because of it."*

Nick Davis reported at the time:

> *"I remember joining the convoy somewhere in the West Country on the Friday evening and travelling on a big converted coach with a young woman called Rosie and her partner and their young baby. The whole convoy was heading for Stonehenge for a free festival, but as we entered Wiltshire, we started drawing a lot of attention from police, some of whom stopped us to inform us that the festival had been cancelled. I remember thinking how arrogant and strange it was that the police could imagine that they could cancel an event which they had had nothing to do with organising in the first place. That night, the convoy rested in Savernake Forest near Marlborough. There was a lot of talk about whether the police would try to stop them reaching Stonehenge the next day; and a lot of wild-eyed crazy stuff about how the sun and the moon would protect them.*

> *Sometime in the early afternoon the next day, the police did indeed try to stop them. Early in the morning, the Observer photographer and I had driven the route trying to guess where the police would make their stand, looking for places where the road was flanked by deep ditches or steep banks to stop the convoy vehicles manoeuvring. We found several likely places. In the event, for whatever reason, the police blocked the road, in a place where it was easy for the convoy to burst out sideways, into the famous bean field.*

> *All that afternoon, there was a stand-off. More and more police arriving. There was some tension among the travellers in the field. I tried to act as middleman to negotiate some kind of peaceful solution, but the police were not interested: everybody in the field had to surrender to be arrested. It was clear that the police had had enough of the convoy making them look silly; and possible that they had deliberately stopped them in a place where they could break free, in order to justify being able to attack and arrest everybody involved. Early in the evening, the police – all togged up in riot gear – entered the field. The convoy vehicles started to move, circling around the field, trying to evade capture.*

> *Soon, it became quite violent – some vehicles on fire, men and women being dragged across the field. At one point, I saw Rosie and her baby being taken away. There was a police helicopter overhead, barking encouragement to the officers on the ground. It felt very upsetting, an act of organised bullying. My photographer was arrested – for taking pictures. There*

came a point when there was only one vehicle still free – a big old coach, known I think as the Rasta Bus – which was careering round in circles, with the police chasing. Eventually, they cornered it and went steaming in. I saw them hauling out a young lad with blood pouring down his face. It was all pretty nasty. And for what? To stop young people making music."

Painting the Peace Convoy bus.

1986

20 – 22 June

The festival grew again this year which required additions to the farm office, communications, welfare and medical teams. The Theatre and Children's Areas moved to new homes and 1985 saw the arrival of the first classical music tent. The main market and the market area relocated to the top of the site. This year attendance topped 60,000, paying £17 for entry and the programme costing a £1, the same price the first revellers paid for entry only fifteen years earlier. £130,000 was raised for CND and other local charities. The acts included: The Cure, Madness, Simply Red, The Housemartins, The Waterboys, Pogues and Level 42.

1986 saw many more travellers at the festival to celebrate the summer solstice now that the exclusion zone was well in force around Stonehenge. The festival was by this time beginning to evolve into diverse cultures with the hippies and environmentalists gathering around the Green Fields and the travellers having their own site.

Edward Palmer Thompson 1924–1993

Thompson was a British historian who played a key role within CND during the 1980s, speaking at innumerable meetings and events such as The Glastonbury Festival. 1986 was not his first appearance at the festival. He devoted a great deal of time to his commitment and was a major influence in opening discussions between the West European peace movement and Soviet-dominated Eastern Europe.

Admission now costs £17.

E. P. Thompson speaking at the festival 1986.

Madness they call it Madness

The link to CND was not unanimously supported by the festival organisers as many had closer bonds with the festival's spiritual background, many unimpressed with the replacement of the sun atop the Pyramid stage although still simply called 'stage one' at this time, with the CND logo. A principal reason for Madness appearing at the 1986 festival was their association with CND having previously played at the National CND rally in 1985.

Madness were one of the main attractions, a statement backed up by their coverage in the festival programme, including a full page interview with Suggs, a full page advert of the band's association with CND and a biography of the band. Their set was scheduled for 7pm on the Sunday night following Simply Red. This period in the festival history is one of conflict between rival factions including drug dealers, and security guards, local farmers and land owners, festival goers and travellers. Melvin Bean of Mean Fiddler described this era as having two gangs from Bristol effectively running parts of the site and Anarco Travellers. Decent hippie travellers didn't get a look in … there were no-go areas … it was a free for all. The perimeter fence was still only partially enclosing the site at this time so anyone just had to walk around the edge to get in, so with no security it left the bands on stage vulnerable.

Madness played 19 tracks that night including, it was said, 'Grey Day' just in case it rained, but thankfully the sun shone.

The full set list was: *Take It Or Leave It, Baggy Trousers, Precious One, Michael Caine, Grey Day, My Girl, Tomorrow's Dream, House Of Fun, Yesterday's Man, Night Boat To Cairo, Time, It Must Be Love, Shut Up, I'll Compete, Embarrassment, Our House. Encore: Madness, The Harder They Come, One Step Beyond.*

The Jimmy-Cliff-penned track, 'The Harder They Come', had a rare outing as it is believed to have been the only time they played it at a gig until its release in 1992

Their set coincided with the infamous England v Argentina football match, the first since the Falkland's War with Argentina winning 2-1 courtesy of the famous 'Hand of God' goal from Diego Maradona, with Suggs keeping the crowd up to date with the score. Lee recalls:

> *"Our crew truck with backline (instruments) was nowhere to be found forty minutes before we were due on. The rest of the band had arrived and our tour manager Huw was looking slightly tense, as he approached me and asked if the worse came to the worse would I mind using someone else's saxophone. But of course I didn't mind, a sax is a sax, anyhow I had absolute confidence in the road crew, Rob, and Toks, they hadn't missed turning up at a show without equipment ever (well except Sydney, May 86). The sun popped its hat on for the forty or so minutes we were on stage. The crowd seemed to go on forever, many of them at the back constantly on the move, rather strange seeing this, I didn't realise there were so many real hippies left on the planet."*

Poster from the 1986 programme and event list for the Sunday night on stage 1, 2 and 3.

1987

19 – 21 June

Would it take place? Mendip District Council had refused permission to grant a licence for this year's festival but it did go ahead as the council decision was overturned in court but not until May. For the first time numbers would fall as a limit of 55,000 was imposed by the council. Mendip Council had sanctioned aerial photography to estimate the number at the previous year's festival and they claimed over 80,000 were on site, but this was proved not to be the case when the footage was studied. The official attendance was recorded at 60,000 but the actual figure was debatable as many had again gained entry as fence-crashers. This year's festival had an uncomfortable ending with the convoy of travellers testing the organisation's patience to the limit. From the festival's early beginnings Michael had always accommodated the travellers with free entry for their convoy of vehicles. Michael explained:

"I've worked with the convoy and with travellers over the years, negotiated with them one-to-one, accommodated them when I could or when I've had to. My approach is a bit different to English Heritage's, isn't it? We do feel that we are not in the position to stage a free festival here, even though that's what we did in 1986 in order to keep a dialogue going with the travellers. We had several thousand people here that didn't pay to come in, but somehow we managed to cope.

When it became known that the convoy were coming to us instead of Stonehenge the council at Mendip got worried, understandably so. News at Ten and BBC news were causing us problems, saying it was like the end of the world, medieval brigands, etc. I was saying, well we've had people like this for years.

But in order to pacify everyone we had to stage a TV show of the convoy leaving. So we were seen to be sorting out the problems and made a case for looking after women and children. In the end all the worries and fears melted away and we managed to keep going!"

The 1987 festival was seen as a major step of diversification from a traditional rock festival to a more multi-national lifestyle affair including the introduction of the WOMAD stage. For many the roots of the free Stonehenge-type festival was replaced with a more commercial venture, it had to be to move on and grow. According to some reports it was estimated that as many as 450 travellers' vehicles were present, all accommodated on a lay-up site adjacent to the Festival.

Reports of trouble at the festival varied depending on the perspective but the travellers claimed that urban drug gangs selling hard drugs had muscled in on their traditional cuisine of hallucinogenic mushrooms and cannabis. Other accounts told of travellers looting and hassling festival staff. The traditional travellers were now joined by a minority who used less than peaceful methods to achieve their aims.

The festival would not go ahead in 1988 and some cited this and the fact that many of the original staff had parted company. With the break the organisers and the farm had some time to recover.

WOMAD

"WOMAD had a couple of bad years financially so I thought perhaps they might like to do a franchise arrangement with us. They're very good at booking good African bands and we were good at chasing after the latest fashionable bands and all the other stuff we were trying to cope with. So I arranged to meet Thomas Brooman at Carwardine's coffee shop in Park Street, Bristol.

I made the proposal to employ his team to run our World Music stage and to call it the WOMAD stage. I would pay him a booking fee to provide us with an excellent programme. I think it was £12,000. It worked well for us and as a result the Womad crew had lots of similar bookings at other events – particularly Roskilde in Denmark.

After a couple of years he naturally wanted more money for their efforts but I couldn't handle doubling of the fee, and a reminder to him that this franchising idea was in any case my suggestion didn't cut any ice.

So we unfortunately parted company and went back to what we did before. That stage was known as Jazz/World until 2010 when it became West Holts (which is the name of the field). It has now become one of the most popular stages on site."

Michael Eavis

Elvis Costello.

Left: *Julie Felix.*

Previous pages: *The camp site, the Pyramid stage and Glastonbury Tor.*

Billy Bragg with Brendan Croker.

1989

16 – 18 June

Once again there were complications with Mendip District Council's granting of the festival licence. The police were bought into the organisation and planning of the Festival for the first time. The licence was for 65,000 but an estimated 100,000 were in attendance, many in the travellers' field for their own free festival, provided by Michael Eavis as a sanctuary for the travellers with entertainment hosted on 'Wango Riley's' travelling stage, a simple truck with the back cut out to provide the stage. Acts included Hawkwind. The music continued day and night from un-official sound systems that had begun to spring up.

Trouble at the festival was nothing like the levels of 1987, with the police invited to patrol inside for the first time. The site now covered 500 acres and despite the se-curity measures and high fencing encircling the site the fence-jumping continued. The weather was kind this year with the Vale of Avalon very hot and dry, some saying that helped toward a more relaxed festival atmosphere. During this period of the festival the acts booked were quite predictable with a smattering of some less well known performers, reasoning being that the fees payable to the big names would have a detrimental effect on the money available to the charities.

The 1989 ticket price was £28 with the programme price £2.

Donations of £100,000 were made to CND and the acts included: Van Morrison, making his third appearance, The Wonderstuff, Elvis Costello, Pixies, Suzanne Vega, Hothouse Flowers, Donovan, Bhundi Boys, Fairground Attraction, The Pro-claimers and The Blues Band.

Hothouse Flowers with Adam Clayton of U2.

The event leaflet for 1989 Glastonbury CND Festival began with the following statement;

This event at Worthy Farm in the Vale of Avalon has over 1000 acts on 10 stages covering the complete range of contemporary performing arts, and offers a major stimulus to the morale and finance of the Campaign For Nuclear Disarmament. At £28 for the whole weekend this must be by far the best value in the country.

The poster concluded by stating that:

This year the police have been invited by the organisers to patrol the whole site with a view to help prevent crime and drug dealing.

The 1990 festival would take its name from the description in the poster and be known as The Glastonbury Festival for Contemporary Performing Arts.

Croissant Neuf

Originally starting out as a skiffle band in East Anglia, playing pubs, folk festivals and village halls the Croissant Neuf of today was just a dream. All six founder members had a keen interest in performance: music, theatre and circus, and 1986 saw the first Croissant Neuf tent being used as a café/venue at shows around the region. The café originally specialised in selling croissants and coffee and it quickly assumed its distinctive name.

1986 also saw the original Croissant Neuf collective host the Oak Fair – a music festival in Suffolk – and appear for the first time at Glastonbury Festival. Since that appearance Croissant Neuf has become an ever present feature at Glastonbury including 1989, gradually transforming into the 1000 capacity solar-powered venue that sits at the heart of Green Fields today.

Croissant Neuf is one of the most original, innovative and creative constants on the festival scene!

Wango Riley's travelling stage.

Wango Riley's travelling stage, a truck with the sides cut out, performed a sterling service at many free festivals during the 1980s and played host to bands night and day. 1989 was the first year of the impromptu, unofficial, sound systems playing non-stop music, seen by some as a refreshing wind of change, and by others a bloody nuisance.

1990 – 20th Anniversary

22 – 24 June

The festival took the name of the Glastonbury Festival for Contemporary Performing Arts for the first time, to reflect the diversity of attractions within the festival. It was the twentieth anniversary of the first festival but unfortunately ended with a confrontation between the security teams and the travellers. The Battle of Yeoman's Bridge resulted in 235 arrests and £50,000 worth of damage to property and hired plant, and consequently 1991 passing without a festival.

1990 was the first year that a professional car parking team was employed to encourage the best use of space. Donations amounting to £100,000 were made to CND and other local charities.

Acts included: The Cure, Happy Mondays, Sinead O'Connor, Aswad, Deacon Blue and Hothouse Flowers.

Official attendance was 70,000. Tickets cost £38 and the programmes £3.

The change of name marked the last year CND would receive a substantial charitable donation. The nuclear threat had now ebbed, although it would come again, with the emphasis now shifting to environmental issues. The site had grown again to accommodate the growing numbers who had to put up with the seasonal rain showers on the Friday.

The 1990 festival evokes unhappy memories for many. It would be the last year that the travellers would have their own field and gain free entry to the festival. The proceedings got underway acrimoniously with the travellers arriving en masse, forcing many of the ticket-paying revellers to endure a lengthy wait of several hours before they could gain entry to the site. The result was a fracas that saw tempers frayed and many vehicles damaged.

The Battle of Yeoman's Bridge

The festival was overshadowed by an event as it was drawing to a close and many conflicting reports have been written of the incident. One thing was for sure – it changed the face of the festival forever. It was said that the new security team took a very heavy hand and the atmosphere within the travellers' field was very tense. It all started to kick off on the Monday when many of the crowd had left and the travellers started to pick over the rubbish left behind.

The consequences have been described by many as a full-on battle. Who started the fight and who was the most violent is not an issue that should be discussed here but the fallout from that day would prevent the 1991 festival going ahead. When it was resurrected in 1992 the site was encircled with a ten foot high fence and an exclusion zone set up, much like 'Stonehenge' had witnessed a few years earlier with the travellers told to go away. Although Michael still continued to employ some travellers that he could trust, the free festival was no longer an option. The Battle of Yeoman's Bridge dominated the festival even though for three days beforehand over 70,000 had enjoyed the music and contemporary arts as promised in advance by the event posters.

Michael was quoted as saying:

> *"The trouble started because one guy was drunk and drove his truck through some fences and stole a tent belonging to the church, it wasn't abandoned, so if this is true, this was a case of theft. Security intervened and cracked his windscreen in the process. We don't know how heavy handed they actually were in their dealings with the drunk, but he wasn't actually injured. The police came and took him away, again apparently unscathed and his van was towed off to a safe spot in the festival grounds, but some kids from the field who had witnessed the arrest ran off to the travellers field and reported that he had been beaten up by security."*

The news, as would be expected, was met by anger from a section of the travellers and they raced to the scene to seek revenge for the treatment he had seemingly received.

Opposite: Watercolour impression of a traveller's home on site.

A tranquil scene in the horse drawn zone on the travellers' field

Traveller Dave

1992

26 – 28 June

After a year off to re-group, the 1992 festival took on a new phase with the profits this year being donated to Greenpeace and Oxfam. Michael Eavis had felt that with the ending of the Cold War, concern had moved away from the diminishing treat of nuclear war, to what was happening to the environment. The festival was also linked with National Music Day and a staggering £250,000 was donated to Greenpeace, Oxfam and other local charities.

A crowd of 70,000 paid £49 each to gain entry and the cost of the programme had now reached £4.

1992 saw the festival morph as many have said, some feeling that its humble beginnings were now a distant memory with the travellers now excluded and the introduction of several new initiatives to what was described as a bigger and better Festival. One being the introduction of the Jazz World stage, and another a 'special surprise guest' on the Sunday. As would be expected rumours abounded as to who that would be: could it be U2 or maybe Prince. When Tom Jones was announced the air was said to be filled with disappointment. The sudden cancellation by Morrissey, who claimed that he had problems with a member of the band, was not helped by the replacement, James.

The line up featured Joan Armatrading, The Blue Aeroplanes, Blur, Billy Bragg And The Red Stars, The Breeders, Carter, The Unstoppable Sex Machine, Hugh Cornwell, Curve, Dr Phibes And The House Of Wax Equations, The Faith Healers, The Fall, The Family Cat, Fat Dinosaur, Fishbone, Flowered Up, The Frank And Walters, Buddy Guy, PJ Harvey, The House Of Love, James, Mazlyn Jones, Tom Jones, K Passa, Kitchens Of Distinction, The Levellers, Kirsty MacColl, Midway Still, Van Morrison, Yossou N'Dour, Ned's Atomic Dustbin, Ocean Colour Scene, The Orb, Primal Scream, The Real People, Lou Reed, Runrig, The Saw Doctors, Senseless Things, Senser, Shakespear's Sister, The Shamen, Spiritualized, Television, Richard Thompson, Thousand Yard Stare, Chris Whitley, and Jah Wobble's Invaders Of The Heart.

Glastonbury Festival
of Contemporary Performing Arts

26-27-28 June 1992

in association with NME NEW MUSICAL EXPRESS

▲ INTRODUCTION ▲

So we're back again, with renewed energy and enthusiasm after a gap of two years, to create what we expect will be one of the most exciting events in Europe this summer. The rest has given us an opportunity to increase our local support — so much so that Mendip District Council have approved the Festival licence with a generous 14-6 in favour.

After ten years of fund-raising for CND — with a great deal of success — we have now decided to shift our efforts towards supporting Greenpeace. Whilst I appreciate that much has still to be done for the anti-nuclear cause, I believe the message has now got through to the majority and, thank God, politicians are at last moving towards the goals we have all been striving for. Greenpeace's environmental focus represents the issues which will dominate the nineties and the consciousness of young people coming to this festival through the next decade.

We are sorry to have to raise the ticket price yet again: inflation would have brought it to £47, but the need to comply with the new Code of Practice for outdoor concerts demands that we erect a 10'6" steel fence around the whole site — a total of 4 miles — and this brings it to £49. We think this still represents good value, considering what the festival has to offer.

Michael Eavis

▶ MUSIC

As always, the best of contemporary music from anywhere in the world. Five music stages will cover headliners, indie bands, acoustic, jazz and world music. By popular demand, Stage 2 has been reincarnated as the NME stage, and will help to reduce the crowding problems at the Pyramid.

▶ THEATRE, MIME, DANCE & CABARET

In the Theatre Field there will be **non-stop cabaret from 10.30am until 2.00am** each day in the enormous **Cabaret Marquee**. The **Serious Marquee** will host at least five major shows each day — the best of theatre, mime and dance from England and overseas. The **second Theatre Marquee** and the **Outside Theatre Stage** will offer a huge variety of theatre shows, poetry, puppets, etc., and the field will be full of **music sculptures, clowns, wandering performers** and some **major European 'street' shows**.

▶ NEW CIRCUS

A huge **1,000-seat Big Top** will host the major circus acts and there will be a **second Circus Marquee** and **Outside Circus Stage** offering a huge variety of New Circus. In addition the field will be full of special events: stunning shows on the **high wire** and the **flying trapeze** accompanied by **pyrotechnics**; the weird and wonderful **Wheel of Death; Bunjie Jumpers; Strong Men; Escapologists; Trampolinists** and **Human Cannonballs. Acrobats, stilt-walkers** and wandering circus performers will abound, and there will also be chances for you to ride the **Mechanical Bull**, the **Gyrating Gyroscope**, the **Velcro Wall** and even fly on a trapeze, as well as join in juggling and other circus skills workshops.

▶ GREENFIELD

The Green Field '92 offers old friends and new an opportunity to come together to share new age visions and concerns:- the environment; green politics; alternative healing; astrology and divination; diverse crafts; music and dance; wholefoods; etc.

Rainbow Circle Village; Green Deserts; Green Futures; the local Glastonbury-inspired **Field of Avalon; Sacred Space** in King's Ground (no camping); **Alternative Technology;** the **Healing Area** and the **Green Trading Market** are some of the focal areas.

Within this framework there will be a quieter space within the main Festival for you to meet like-minded souls and explore new skills and relationships to the planet and to one another. Come and join us!

▶ CINEMA

This year there will be two cinema screens: the big outdoor screen will be running from about 10.30pm each night, showing popular general release films — **Dances with Wolves, Thelma and Louise, Ghost, The Commitments** and **Robin Hood** to name but a few. The second screen will be in a marquee and thus be able to play all day as well, and will be showing more 'art' movies, such as **Cyrano de Bergerac, Miller's Crossing, Romuald and Juliet** and **The Field.** It is being programmed and staffed with the help of the Edinburgh Festival Film Guild, the BFI and other members of the BFFS.

Both screens will be running 35mm projectors, and the outside venue will be in Dolby stereo with surround sound. The portable projectors and sound system have been loaned to the festival by Cinema Supply and Design of Milton Keynes.

● A Message from Greenpeace ●

Greenpeace welcomes its new association with the festival and is planning a dramatic presence! Although we intend to come in from the skies — as part of a major campaign to save the ozone layer — you will find us on the ground in a marquee. Above our heads a hole in the ozone layer is looming due to the chemical pollution of our skies. Greenpeace is campaigning to stop the hole and save the ozone layer.

Meet us at Glastonbury at the edge of the hole.

▶ CHILD'S PLAY

Admission is free for children under 14, and as always there will be a Festival within a Festival for the young and the young at heart, centred on the **adventure playground**. Performances at three separate venues through the day, **face-painting, craft workshops, inflatables, rides, donkeys, games,** and a **fenced-in sanctuary** for the smaller children, all staffed by plenty of adults, make sure that there's loads of fun in store for everyone. This year we will be throwing the stage open to the children themselves, with a **talent show every day** (max. age 18), and workshops to develop performance skills of all kinds. At 7pm we close down so that tired children can have dinner and a good night's sleep.

▶ MARKETS

There is a wonderful selection of colourful market stalls: in **Place de Babylon, Las Shamblas, Chalice Way** or **the Souk,** you can buy anything from Biafran *haute cuisine* to fresh flowers or beautifully made jewellery — watch out for Café Bordel and the best farmhouse ice cream in Britain. If you have anything very special to sell,

write to Magnus, c/o Worthy Farm, Pilton, Shepton Mallet, Somerset, BA4 4BY, with details.

▶ SITE ACCESS

The site will be open from 9am on Wednesday 24th June, before which time no one but traders will be allowed in. This year there will be more car parking next to the site where **no camping will be allowed.** Caravans and caravanettes will be placed in a separate field, but close to the site. A **premium of £50** will be charged to cover some of the costs of this facility.

▶ ANIMALS

The Festival is not a suitable place to bring animals of any kind, be they dogs, cats, horses or goats.

▶ GETTING TO THE SITE

The site is in the village of Pilton, on the A361 between Glastonbury and Shepton Mallet. Approach via the M4/M5: exit at jnct. 23 (M5). Then follow the A39 through Glastonbury. From there the route is clearly signposted. If travelling by rail, the nearest station is Castle Cary, from where there will be a free coach service to and from the site. There are also Badgerline coaches from Bristol and Bath. National Express are organising coach services from all over the country.

☎ INFORMATION LINE

The INFO line is now open providing up to the minute information on performers and travel to and from the Festival site:

INFORMATION line:
0839-66 88 99*.

*Calls charged at 36p per min. cheap rate — 48p per min. at other times.

■ TICKETS

Admission to the festival is again by **advance ticket only.** Camping, car parking, V.A.T. and all on-site events are included in the ticket price. Children under 14 are admitted free.

We expect demand for tickets will be heavy, so apply early to be sure to get in! Tickets are £49 and can be obtained from:–

Direct — **no commission:**
By phone — ticket information and credit cards:
0272 767 868
By post:
Glastonbury Festivals Ltd. (Ticket Unit), PO Box 903, Bristol BS99 5ND

Do **not** enclose a stamped addressed envelope. If you want your ticket(s) sent by **registered post** please add £2 per order (not per ticket). Cheques & postal orders should be made payable to **Glastonbury Festivals Ltd.** Please allow 21 days for delivery. Postal applications cannot be accepted after June 7th.

Tickets can also be obtained in person from the **CND shop** at **162 Holloway Road, London N7,** and usual outlets throughout the country — details will appear in the music press.

By coincidence National Music Day falls on the same weekend as the Festival — musical events of all kinds are scheduled throughout the country. We are pleased to be able to contribute to its success.

National Music Day

Festival Dragons – Ray Brooks

"In 1992 I was asked by Michael Eavis to build a Fire Dragon for the Glastonbury Festival. This was followed over the next three years by the dragons of Earth, Air and Water. I was assisted by many people, especially Sara Munroe and Mark Copeland, who built the flying Air Dragon in 1994, Roger Bloomfield , Mary, Anna, Carole and all who helped create the Water Dragon, and Dave Starkey with The Earth Dragon. Thanks to them and all the many others who helped."

The Elemental Dragons:

"Hidden in our minds, there are Dragons…"

Dragons are a racial memory, an expression of the primeval relationship between Man-Earth-Universe. They can make connections to the Infinite Universe and the Subconscious as Powers, Guiding Forces, and angels of the Goddess. These Elemental Dragons have emerged from a strange mixture of Chinese Legends, Medicine Wheel Teachings, Celtic Mythology and the Power of Breath.

But mostly from the Imagination. Each of the Elemental Dragons has Qualities.

The Earth Dragon, for example, is the Dragon of the South and of summer. His colours are Red and Green. His animal is the Mouse and his plant the Rose. Some of his Qualities are: Energy, Vitality, Growth and Creativity.
He is involved in Making Changes with Love and Compassion.

He is Trust and Innocence. Each of us also has our Personal Dragon, or Dragons, who may help or hinder – they have a refreshing sense of humour and they teach us.

All is open to interpretation. Nothing is fixed, Thought is Creative.

The Story Of How We Made The Dragons

The cycle of Elemental Dragons at Glastonbury began in 1992. At the top of the festival site, above the Green Areas, is King's Meadow, a field that has become known as the Sacred Space, an area of retreat and reflection. It is the site of the Stone Circle, the Totem and many rituals, songs, dances and weirdness for many years. I was asked to create a Fire Dragon there. And so began the Dragon circle. It has turned into a way of seeing, experiencing and celebrating the presence of Dragons in the World. Each year for four years a dragon was built – a full turn of the wheel.

The Fire Dragon
She was built from welded steel and aluminium – 60 feet in length. Inside her belly was space for twenty people to sit around a huge egg-shaped kiln. Seven slender shining chimney pipes, 20 feet high, carried away the smoke. The egg became a roaring furnace for

four days and four nights. It contained a new, baby dragon, made from water and clay. Eventually the fire faded and the egg cracked open and crumbled leaving the fired ceramic dragon amongst the ashes.

That night the Fire Dragon breathed gouts of flame across the field and herself burst into a mighty conflagration. When all was cooled and the festival was over, people came and took away pieces of the fired clay dragon and so he was scattered and journeyed in many directions.

The Earth Dragon
He took the form of a huge clay kiln over 50 feet long. It was designed to fire itself from within. First, Hazel saplings were cut from the hedges and freshly coppiced withies brought from the lowland withy beds in West Zoyland. A large pit was excavated and the shape of the dragon woven in wicker over the frame. The whole was then covered in layers of paper, clay slip, and a mixture of clay and straw.

The Earth Dragon had returned. He lay drying in the sun for many days. The fire was lit and soon he breathed smoke and flames into the Air. Eventually the fierce fire hardened and scorched his skin. Then a shock. The circle turned – in a storm of sparks and fire the Dragon collapsed, sank into the Earth, and left. No trace now remains in the grass of the field.

The Air Dragon
The following year, spurred perhaps by a lick of flame the Air Dragon flew in from the East. He was made from fabric, wood, and delicate Willow. 40 feet long and suspended high in a tall framework of tree-trunks. He hovered thoughtfully in the Air throughout the festival, rising and falling gracefully in the wind, nudged into more erratic movement by passers-by.

As the people began to leave he too departed. His observations complete he continued on his journey to the East, carrying the breath of autumn in his wings.

The Water Dragon
Then the Water Dragon, flying in from the North, chose a place to settle, a new pond on the stream. Over 80 feet long, built on a wood and welded steel framework, with thick layers of concrete and stone gathered from the farm, sliced rocks, crystals and gems. She, of all four dragons, is the one to stay, blending herself in with the passage of time, a channel for the water, a home for the mosses and lichens and perhaps a refuge for small damp creatures.

There has been great Power, Joy, Hard Work, Fear and Discovery in this journey. What it was all about I've still to discover. Lots of odd stories to tell.

The Fire Dragon – Worthy Farm Pilton Glastonbury Festival 1992.

1993

25 – 27 June

The attendance for this year's festival reached a new milestone with 80,000 paying a record £58 each for entry to the three day event. The festival was now taking on its modern appearance, becoming a worldwide phenomenon. The golden oldie theme having begun the previous year was continued with the appearance of Rolf Harris, complete with his 'Wobble Board'. Greenpeace, Oxfam and local charities continued to benefit from donations of £250,000.

The 1993 festival like 1992 enjoyed another hot dry year. The attractions continued to grow with music, theatre, comedy, cabaret, cinema and circus all now permanent features of the Glastonbury Festival of Contemporary Performing Arts.

The Pyramid stage featured the likes of Midnight Oil, Velvet Underground, Robert Plant, Alison Moyet, The Kinks, Van Morrison and the golden oldie Rolf Harris.

The second stage (The NME stage) featured Jamiroqui, Stereo MCs, Lemonheads and The Orb.

The Jazz stage showcased James Taylor, Roy Ayres and Urban Species.

The Acoustic stage echoed to the sounds of Donovan, Lindisfarne and Nanci Griffith.

A fuller but not comprehensive list of acts from the festival promotion poster included:

Lenny Kravitz, Van Morrison, Jamiroquai , Underground, James, Primal Scream, The Black Crowes, The Kinks, Michael Franti & Spearhead, Suede, Donovan, Robert Plant, The Lemonheads, Midnight Oil, Stereo MCs, Billy Bragg, The Orb, Teenage Fanclub, The Tragically Hip, Roy Ayers, Sebadoh, Superchunk, Porno for Pyros, Belly, Nanci Griffith, American Music Club, Eddi Reader, Ozric Tentacles, Tim Finn, Rolf Harris, The Auteurs, Lindisfarne, Sharon Shannon, Leatherface, D'influence, Green On Red, Galliano, The 4 of Us, The God Machine, Mega City Four, John Otway, The Coal Porters, Ultramarine, The Blues Band, Fun Da Mental, Planet, The Rocking Birds and Bronte Brother.

The festival had a distinctive late '60s feel with Donovan, Ray Davies of The Kinks and Robert Plant.

Michael Eavis said *"this year's festival was probably the best one we've ever had, it's the second one without the travellers which has made a lot of difference."* The travellers had been kept away by police this year in an effort to avoid any confrontation from the fallout of the 1990 festival, events that contributed to no festival in 1991.

An unfortunate incident that resulted in serious injury would force Michael to tighten security for the next year by installing a double fence around the site to prevent gate-crashers (or fence-crashers as they are known) in an attempt to ensure the crowd limit was not breached.

On the Acoustic stage the crowd were treated to a set by Lindisfarne who had a revival of their '70s hits *Fog On The Tyne* in 1990 with a little help from a famous Geordie footballer.

Lindisfarne

The group began as the Downtown Faction, but soon changed their name to Brethren in 1968, after hearing of an American group of the same name; they were re-christened Lindisfarne after the island off the Northumbrian coast. The original ine-up was Ray Jackson, Alan Hull, Ray Laidlaw, Rod Clements and Simon Cowe.

In 1970 they signed to Charisma Records and their debut album *Nicely Out Of Tune* (so named because the group claimed they were nicely out of tune with other prevailing musical trends at the time) was released, defining their mixture of bright harmony and rollicking folk rock. Both singles released from their album, *Clear White Light* and *Lady Eleanor*, failed to chart, as did the album itself at first. Nonetheless, the band obtained a strong following from its popular live concerts. Their second album, *Fog On The Tyne*, followed in 1971 and began their commercial success, charting late in 1971 and reaching number one the following year. Their profile was also raised when Jackson played mandolin on Rod Stewart's breakthrough hit single *Maggie May*, even though Stewart only credited him on the sleeve of the parent album *Every Picture Tells a Story* as "the mandolin player in Lindisfarne, the name slips my mind." For years the legend persisted that disc jockey John Peel had played the mandolin part, solely because he was invited to mime it on *Top of The Pops*.

Top ten singles *Meet Me OnThe Corner,* written by Clements, and a re-release of *Lady Eleanor,* followed in 1972, and *Nicely Out Of Tune* belatedly made the top ten. The band obtained a huge media following, with some calling Hull the greatest songwriter since Bob Dylan, and the band was even referred to as the '1970s' Beatles'.

Internal tensions came to the fore during a disappointing tour of Australia in early 1973. Hull initially considered leaving the band, but was persuaded to reconsider. It was agreed that he and Jackson, the two joint lead vocalists, would keep the group name while Cowe, Clements, and Laidlaw left to form their own outfit, Jack The Lad. They were replaced by Tommy Duffy (bass guitar), Kenny Craddock (keyboards), Charlie Harcourt (guitar), and Paul Nichols (drums). Ray said:

> *"I was never going to be a part of the Hull and Jackson led Lindisfarne Mk 2. When they knew I wasn't interested they approached Phil Collins and when he declined they hired Paul Nichols."*

In 1977 they reformed, and with a new record deal with Phonogram Records. They were back in the charts in 1978 with the top ten hit *Run For Home,* an autobiographical song about the rigours of touring and relief at returning home. It gave them a top forty hit in the US at last, and the album *Back and Fourth* made the British top thirty.

In the '80s, throughout various line up changes, they continued to release albums, with only their nostalgic live recordings achieving any real attention, recording singles like *I Must Stop Going To Parties* on their own Lindisfarne Musical Productions label in the mid '80s, as well as one album, *Sleepless Nights*. In 1984 they supported Bob Dylan and Santana at St James' Park, home of their beloved Newcastle United FC. Saxophone player and vocalist Marty Craggs joined the group shortly afterwards. Throughout the '80s and early '90s they played annual Christmas tours. *C'mon Everybody* was a double vinyl LP consisting largely of old rock'n'roll standards, such as the title track, *Party Doll*, and *Twist and Shout.*

In 1990 they introduced themselves to a new generation when a duet of *Fog On The Tyne Revisited* with footballer Paul Gascoigne rose to number two in the UK singles chart. Ray added:

> *"…after Alan Hull's sudden death in 1995, the band continued with Billy Mitchell fronting, and they made two more albums, one produced by ex-Long Ryder Sid Griffin, before finally calling it a day in 2003."*

Lindisfarne at Glastonbury.

1994

24 – 26 June

In the early hours on the 13 June a mysterious fire razed the Pyramid stage to the ground and a replacement was made available by the same company that supplied the NME and Jazz stages. This year's festival offered both innovation and tragedy. Channel 4 televised the event live over the weekend opening it up to a much wider audience and a wind turbine was set up to provide power for the main stage arena. Armed police had to be called in when a man started firing a pistol during a fight on the Saturday involving five people and the festival witnessed its first death due to a drugs overdose the same night, the first in the twenty-four year history of the festival.

Michel Eavis reported, *"There has been more violence this year than we've ever had before, but the overriding mood is one of a peaceful event."* The attendance just about topped the 80,000 and entry had increased by a £1 on the previous year to £59 with the festival programme selling at £5. As in the past couple of years the beneficiaries from the weekend event shared a staggering £250,000 with Greenpeace and Oxfam each receiving £100,000 and local charities and good causes receiving £50,000.

The line up:

The temporary 'Pyramid stage' featured on the Friday: The Levellers, Rage Against The Machine, Beck, Saint Etienne, Blind Melon and World Party.

Saturday saw Elvis Costello, James, Grant Lee, Buffalo and Ride.

Sunday saw Peter Gabriel, Johnny Cash, Tendersticks and Mary Black graced the stage.

Over on the NME stage the weekend's performers included: The Pretenders, Manic Street Preachers, Boo Radleys, Beastie Boys, Orbital, Bjork, M People, Blur, Radiohead, Pulp and Echobelly.

The Acoustic stage showcased The Bootleg Beatles.

Beatle mania arrived in the London's West End from Broadway in 1979 when four British hopefuls, Neil Harrison, Andre Barreau, David Catlin-Birch and Jack Lee-Elgood became the UK cast for a major show. The show closed in 1980 and The Bootleg Beatles were formed. In 1994 The Bootleg Beatles headlined the Acoustic stage for the first time watched by members of Oasis and Blur. The same year they completed a two month European tour that culminated at the Albert Hall. Next year they would be back gracing the main stage.

Johnny Cash

Cash wrote that his reception at the 1994 Glastonbury Festival was one of the highlights of his career. Entering on stage in front of jam-packed crowd on a sunny Sunday he looked out in disbelief, went up to the microphone and said those renowned words *"Hello. I'm Johnny Cash,"* the band struck up with *Folsom Prison Blues* and a legendary Glastonbury performance had begun.

The set-list that day was: *Folsom Prison Blues, Sunday Morning Coming Down, I Guess Things Happen That Way, Delia's Grove, Let The Train Blow The Whistle, Big River, Orange Blossom Special, A Boy Named Sue, Get Rhythm, Ring Of Fire, Cash Talks, The Beast In Me, Bird On A Wire, Jackson (a duet with his wife)*

Watercolour impression of the temporary main stage and the wind turbine providing power for the first time.

*Sunday morning 6am and a party is still going
on near the milk tent close to the Cinema Field.*

The 1994 programme now costing
£5 and still an additional expense.

GLASTONBURY FESTIVAL

of Contemporary Performing Arts • 24-25-26 June 1994

The radio recordings made by the BBC at last year's Festival were broadcast in over 45 countries, including China, and were listened to by up to 500 million people. This is a far cry from those early days when Marc Bolan played to less than 1,000 people, in a field next to the farmhouse, with free milk being ladled out from churns in the dairy.

On a less romantic note, in order to effectively control numbers, we are now having to build a second perimeter fence, which will make it virtually impossible to break in: so please, don't come here without a ticket – buy it in advance.

An astonishing array of talent from all around the world is lining up for this year's event – stronger again (if you believe us!) than last year.

Four hundred acres of camping; 160 acres of imaginative and inventive activities of every kind. You have to see it to believe...

– Michael Eavis

in association with

NME NEW MUSICAL EXPRESS and BBC RADIO ONE 97-99 FM

— A Message from GREENPEACE —

WARNING
RADIOACTIVE FACILITY
SELLAFIELD
EXCLUSION ZONE
React!
GREENPEACE

Irish rock group U2 protesting at Sellafield with Greenpeace against the new THORP reprocessing plant

At the beginning of 1994, 500 anti-nuclear protesters from all over the UK and abroad gathered for a day-long vigil outside the High Court in London to mark the opening of Greenpeace's legal action against the Government's decision to grant an operating licence for THORP, British Nuclear Fuel's new reprocessing plant at Sellafield.

Greenpeace's court case was the culmination of a two-year intensive campaign, which observers in Government and the press have described as 'changing the face of environmental protest.' The campaign relied on the generosity of Michael and Jean Eavis, who, through the Glastonbury Festival, have donated over £300,000 to Greenpeace over the last two years. So when you buy your festival ticket this year, remember you will also be supporting Greenpeace!

◀ ★ T·I·C·K·E·T·S ★ ▶

Admission is again by **advance ticket only.** We expect demand to be heavy, so apply early to be sure to get in! **Tickets are £59** and can be obtained directly from the Festival (and from usual ticket outlets).
By phone (ticket info and credit card sales): **0272 767 868.**
By post: Glastonbury Festivals Ltd., PO Box 352, Bristol BS99 7FQ. (No SAE required.)
Camping, car parking, V.A.T. and all on-site events are included in the ticket price. Children under 14 *accompanied by an adult* are admitted free.

● **Please add £2 per ticket** to cover handling and p&p. Cheques & postal orders should be made payable to Glastonbury Festivals Ltd. Allow 21 days for delivery. Postal applications cannot be accepted after June 7th.
● The **INFO line** is now open providing up-to-the-minute information on performers and travel to and from the Festival site: **0839-66 88 99.** Calls are charged at 36p per min. cheap rate – 48p per min. at other times.
● For press enquiries, please phone (0749) 890566.

♻ Recycled paper

● Please don't bring dogs or other animals to the festival – they won't be admitted ●

The festival poster warns not to come without a ticket and please do not bring animals as they will not be admitted.

1995 – 25th Anniversary

23 – 25 June

Over 1000 acts and 17 stages, declared the poster for the 25th anniversary year, a mammoth metamorphosis from those humble beginnings back in the summer of 1970.

The 25th anniversary saw the return of two performers from the inaugural Pilton Pop, Folk and Blues Festival: Keith Christmas and Al Stewart. For the first time the event was sold out within four weeks of the tickets becoming available – how things had moved on. To some extent for many it was a return to the days of the free festival, as the fence was torn down, an act that did not help the feelings of variance with neighbouring landowners. Channel 4 were back to broadcast more entertainment, including some live performances for a growing number of followers.

The festival continued to grow with the introduction of the Dance Tent. Ticket prices now reached £65 and the programme was still a fiver. One of the main headliners The Stone Roses were forced to pull out and were replaced by Pulp. Local charities received £100,000 as did Oxfam with £200,000 donated to Greenpeace. The official attendance for the 25th anniversary was set at 80,000.

The Pyramid stage showcased   The Cure, Oasis, P J Harvey, Simple Minds, whilst the NME stage featured Goldie, Supergrass, Orbital, Prodigy and many more.

Over on the Acoustic stage the crowd were treated to the likes of Portishead, Billy Bragg and Nick Lowe and on the Jazz World stage highlights included Incognito, Gil Scott-Heron and Red Snapper.

The musical variety continued to suit all tastes with Steeleye Span and The Dharmas heard on the Avalon stage.

The Dance Tent

In 1995 Glastonbury received its first dedicated rave-space. It was named, simply, the Dance Tent. This year saw performances from Massive Attack, System 7 and Eat Static. The story of what has become the modern day Glastonbury's Dance Village almost certainly began the previous year with a single performance, one quoted widely as one of the greatest live performances of all time. It was a first-time Glastonbury appearance for two brothers that catapulted dance music into the frame of the festival organisers. Orbital's 1994 performance was both sonically uplifting and visually stunning, as Phil and Paul Hartnoll bounced about the stage in their signature head-torch glasses, to a soundtrack steeped in ambient techno and rave. The following years would see the capacity grow and grow to meet the demands of a flourishing UK dance music scene.

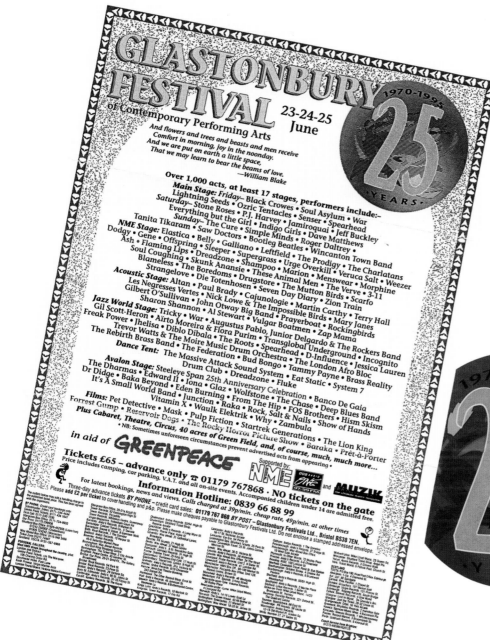

The advertising poster details the plethora of musicians and performers that now graced the festival, celebrating its 25th Anniversary. There would be no festival in 1996 after the phenomenal success of the previous event, to give the farm a rest, the cows the chance to stay out all summer long, and allow all the people involved the chance to take a break from the demands of organising such a large event. August 1996 did however witness the introduction of the Classical Extravaganza at Glastonbury Abbey.

The Cure

"I was there. I had a very strange experience as I went with a bunch of friends and one was a girl that I had recently broken up with and was still very in love with, but fortunately I had a lot of different friends there. The Cure gig was ok but possibly one of my least favourite shows as they came on about 45 minutes late due to going on radio for about an hour, but had to wait as the radio was also covering Bon Jovi at Wembley. Simple Minds were on before The Cure and it was quite funny as people were dancing crazily to them and halfway through the Simple Minds set you could see a sea of black descending towards the stage. The one thing that I remember about this Glastonbury was the best performance I saw that weekend was Pulp who were at the top of their game. Cure wise, and brilliant to hear A Night Like This has always been one of my fave live Cure tracks and I adore Strange Day; also first time I'd heard Jupiter Crash and Mint Car. Guess I was disappointed as I was expecting so much, as the last time they had played Glastonbury it was a legendary gig and because of the of delay coming on they were on for less than two hours, which is short for The Cure. Don't think I've ever seen Robert so angry but they were blinding in parts (well it was The CURE) but were a little out of tune at points."

Jojo Denovan

The Cure formed in Crawley, West Sussex in 1976. The band has experienced several line-up changes, with front-man, vocalist, guitarist and principal songwriter Robert Smith being the only constant member.

1997

27 – 29 June

A spell of torrential rain before, and more downpours during, the weekend saw the 1997 festival dubbed as the 'Year of the Mud'. Undeterred, festival-goers boogied in their boots to more live performances than had ever graced the site. This year's highlights included a 'Carhenge' made from upended VW beetles and campervans, if only they had realised their value today! This year saw the first ever Greenpeace Field, complete with a reconstructed *Rainbow Warrior* and solar-heated showers.

The attendance was officially set at 90,000 although many gained entry through some holes in the fence, though it was reported some left as early as the Saturday. However the vast majority stayed and enjoyed themselves as only festival goers know how. BBC 2's live performances provided a first experience of the festival for many, some no doubt deterred form venturing to future festivals by the sea of mud. A daily newspaper was published by one of the festival sponsors, Select.

The event poster for 1997 was minimalistic and announced 'Legend tells of the enchanted city that appears for just three days a year, at mid-summer, in the flowering meadows of the Vale of Avalon. And 'tis said that there can be found entrancing music, amazing spectacle and strange wonders beyond compare.' Admission was now £75 but did include the programme with Greenpeace, Oxfam, Water Aid and Mid-Somerset CND the main beneficiaries.

The Pyramid stage featured, amongst many, Radiohead with Michael proclaiming *"all time best gig,"* Sting, Van Morrison, The Prodigy, Ray Davies and Cheryl Crow. The other stage featured the likes of Placebo, Ash, Reef, Stereolab and The Chemical Brothers. The Acoustic stage welcomed back The Bootleg Beatles, Billy Bragg and Steve Harley and Cockney Rebel. The original members with Steve Harley were John Crocker and Stuart Elliott, Nick Jones and Paul Jefferys, the latter tragically losing his life along with his bride on their honeymoon on the fateful Pan Am flight blown up over Lockerbie in December 1988.

Their first commercial success in 1972 *Judy Teen* was followed by *Mr Soft*. Their appearance on the legendary John Peel show on Radio One saw the release of a live album. However differences surfaced and by the end of 1972 all the members had quit with the exception of Stuart Elliott. The new band had to wait until 1975 to enjoy chart success with *Make Me Smile (Come Up And See Me)* giving them a number one hit and selling over one million copies worldwide.

Opposite: *The festival is now an event that attracts several sponsors including BBC 2, The Guardian,* Select *magazine and BBC Radio 1 FM.*

27-28-29 June

in aid of

GLASTONBURY FESTIVAL 1997

27·28·29 June

in aid of

GREENPEACE

Legend tells of the enchanted city, which appears for just three days a year, at mid-summer, in the flowering meadows of the Vale of Avalon. And 'tis said that there may be found entrancing music, amazing spectacle and strange wonders beyond compare...

Tickets £75 ☎ 01179 767 868

Info line: 0839 668899

Sponsored by:-

SELECT TheGuardian 2 1FM

The Official Programme of the

1998

26 – 28 June

Mud, Mud Glorious Mud. The rain was back turning the site into a quagmire once more but it failed to deter the diehards who enjoyed the evergreen mix of entertainment from a staggering array of over 1000 performances over the 17 stages with this year seeing a new marquee for up-and-coming bands. The Dance Tent was enlarged and always packed, and the site now boasted a proper on-site bank. This year more than £500,000 was donated to charities, including Greenpeace, Oxfam and Water Aid. The official attendance topped 100,000 with tickets now priced at £80 including a programme. The problem of fence-hoppers continued, and one bizarre incident was reported by Avon and Somerset police at the time telling of two gate-crashers who climbed over the perimeter fence and landed in the police compound where they were arrested for allegedly carrying drugs.

The bands as usual were complemented by jugglers, fire-eaters, poets, and many others. The headline stage was still not officially the Pyramid stage as the distinctive Pyramid shape had yet to be reinstated. The Main stage featured on Friday: Primal Scream, James, Foo Fighters, The Lightning Seeds, Finley Quay, Ben Harper, Taj Mahal, Gomez and My Life Story. Saturday: Blur, Tricky, Robbie Williams, Mansun, Stereophonics, Tori Amos, Hothouse Flowers, Meridith Brooks, Jools Holland and Sharon Shannon. Sunday: Pulp, Nick Cave and The Bad Seeds, Sonic Youth, Bob Dylan, Tony Bennett, Space, Steve Earl, Medieval Babies and The Town Band.

Why so much mud?

Well obviously it rained, and heavily at that. The main site is set in a natural amphitheatre or a valley causing part of the problem. But the real underlying issue is below ground. Dig down a few feet and you will find that the Vale of Avalon is one huge bowl of clay, a waterproof lining with the saturated ground water having nowhere to go. Despite the estimated costs of upward of a million spent on drainage the mud is still an iconic feature of a wet summer in the west of England.

It does make for some very interesting photographs and it seems that it is just an accepted part of the British summer festival scene, some dry years, some wet years and some in between. But it doesn't seem to dampen, excuse the pun, the spirits of the hardy festival goer.

Opposite: *Mud Man. Watercolour impression from an original image.*

1999

25 – 27 June

Downpour precautions were put in place said to have cost £150,000 for the final festival of the twentieth century. However they were not called upon as the sun shone bringing a broad smile to everyone's face, including the performers. The final spectacular before the millennium celebrations, witnessed over 300 bands taking part, an extravaganza of theatre and comedy, and all advertised for the first time on a Glasto website and broadcast live on BBC 2.

This year's event was sadly overshadowed by the death of Michael's wife Jean. A winged wicker sculpture was burned in her honour and fireworks filled the moonlit sky to commemorate her life. Michael said *"Out of respect for Jean's huge input through the years, we called for a minute's silence right across the site at 11.00 in the morning on Sunday 27 June. The stillness was staggering and very emotional."*

The acts on stage this year included Manic Street Preachers, Al Green, Blondie, Pattie Smith and one of John Peel's favourites Lonnie Donegan.

The attendance topped 100,000 with tickets costing £83 including a programme.

The Pyramid stage featured on the Friday: Bjorn Again, Ian Dury, Bare Naked Ladies, Blondie, Bush Hole, Beautiful South and REM.

Saturday: Younger Younger 28s, Billy Bragg, Eliza Carthy, Ben Orton, Joe Strummer, Ash, Texas, Underworld and Manic Street Preachers.

Sunday: London Community Gospel Choir, Delirious, Youthu Yindi, Al Green, The Corrs, Lenny Kravitz, Fun Loving Criminals and Skunk Anansie.

1999 heralded glorious sunsets with 100,000 plus enjoying a great weekend.

The Jazz World stage, the stage covering jazz, hip-hop, soul, and funk, included from the world of reggae, Jazz Jamaica, Ernest Ranglin and Burning Spear. Michael described this year's festival as *"The best Glastonbury yet"*.

The 1999 festival was again overcrowded due to fence-jumpers but nothing like that which followed in 2000 when an estimated 100,0000 gate-crashed, swelling the attendance to an estimated 200,000.

One snippet of hearsay revealed that the Manic Street Preachers requested their own backstage toilets. However it was later revealed by the band that this was a joke; the reserved sign on the toilet was not an official sign.

A gathering of one people, Glastonbury 1999.

A GATHERING OF
ONE PEOPLE

GLASTONBURY FESTIVAL
1999

2000

23 – 25 June

The Pyramid stage was back, with its third incarnation, following the fire of 1997, now a magnificent silver clad monument rising 100 feet high above of the Vale of Avalon. The festival grew once more with the introduction of a family camping area. A new addition for 2000 was The Glade, an outdoor dance venue set on the old railway track amongst the trees in the southeast corner of the site with a capacity to entertain around 4000.

For the 100,000 that paid, the cost of entry was £87 including the obligatory programme. As before, Greenpeace, Oxfam and Water Aid were the main beneficiaries. The perennial gate-crashers turned up again but this time there would be serious repercussions with estimates of well over 200,000 in attendance. Nevertheless the infrastructure stood up to the test and the weekend provided a plethora of entertainment for all tastes.

Public safety concerns and the refusal of another licence would see the festival take the next year off and in March 2001 the Festival was fined £15,000 by Magistrates in Frome from a prosecution by Mendip District Council. £10,000 of that figure was for a noise offence from travellers who stayed on after the event and £5000 for exceeding the crowd limit. The bench did however recognise that Michael has always gone to an enormous amount of trouble to run an efficient and safe festival. The fallow year would be spent carrying out significant work to try to overcome the growing culture of illegal entry thereby ensuring a safe environment for the paying public. It was also reported at the time that many believed the 2001 break was also, in part, a consequence of the 2000 Roskilde accident in which nine people lost their lives during a stage rush. The security for the next festival in two years would be tightened up.

The Pyramid stage featured on Friday: Chemical Brothers, Macy Gray, Counting Crows, Cypress Hill, Bluetones, Live, The Wailers and The Waterboys.

Saturday's line up: Travis, Pet Shop Boys, Ocean Colour Scene, Reef, Semisonic, Brand New Heavies, Asian Dub Foundation, Ladysmith, Black Mambazo and Joseph Arthur.

Sunday: David Bowie, Embrace, Happy Mondays, Willie Nelson, Jools Holland, Sharon Shannon and Yeovil Town Band.

David Bowie's appearance on the main stage was his first since 1971 when he played at the free festival and pledged to put on the show of his life.

The new Pyramid stage rose phoenix-like from the ashes and the glittering 100ft steel structure was erected with a massive footprint of 40m x 40m – four times larger than its previous incarnation. Four kilometres of steel tubing, weighing over 40 tonnes were used in the build, and all materials and processes used passed a Greenpeace environmental audit. This current structure was designed and built by Pilton villager Bill Burroughs, based on the Great Pyramid of Giza in Egypt. It is the most instantly recognised festival stage in the world.

The Glastonbury Festival web site quotes:

"This is where you're going to see the highest profile acts on the bill. In reality, it's the acts that have cost us the most money and whose agents have been insistent that any stage other than Pyramid is out of the question. But what sort of music is played on the Pyramid? Well, it is truly eclectic with the only commonality linking many of the artists being that they are just the best in their field."

David Bowie was foremost amongst them.

David Bowie

2002

28 – 30 June

The most long-awaited and carefully prepared Glastonbury Festival took place in wonderful weather. The ring of steel fence repelled all non-ticket holders and 140,000 legitimate festival goers including 5000 holding Sunday tickets revelled in the space and security created by the widely praised new operational management structure. Tickets were put on sale in February and sold out in weeks. Acts included Stereophonics, Coldplay, Manu Chao, Rolf Harris, Kosheen, Mis-teeq, Fat Boy Slim, Roger Walters, Rod Stewart, White Stripes, Orbital and Isaac Hayes. For many the place to be was Lost Vagueness in the Green Fields which bizarrely provided a silver service restaurant and ballroom dancing. Tickets were now £97 plus a £3 booking fee so had reached the £100 for the first time, with the programme included.

Michael Eavis declared Glastonbury 2002 a 100% success, with a 50% drop in crime and none of the overcrowding problems that dogged previous years and threw the future of the festival into serious jeopardy:

> "We actually got control back again after all these years. The new fence and the campaign, which told people not to come if they didn't have a ticket, was an amazing success. People are starting to respect the event for what it is."

Avon and Somerset Police reported 270 arrests during the event, mostly for robberies and thefts. There were two deaths over the weekend – one, a hit-and-run accident, and the other a man found dead in his tent, although the police did not treat the latter as suspicious. Considering the festival is the size of a small town, when in full swing, these figures are actually surprisingly low. Kept outside the perimeter by the £2m security measures, the ubiquitous criminal element turned their attentions to the local village of Pilton, where a few houses were burgled. Michael Eavis held a vociferous parish meeting to calm local concerns and was confident that the crime problems outside the fence would be resolved next year, allowing the event to go ahead as planned.

Melvin Bean, Managing Director of Mean Fiddler Group, who were drafted in on 20% of the profits to help with the security and administration, said:

> "The people who turned up and caused trouble outside were the criminal element, not festival-goers, and they were out to prey on the customers. It can certainly be said that 2002 saw the Glastonbury Festival put on trial. Fortunately, the case seems to have been adjourned for the moment, and its future is looking rosy. From our experiences, the festival has only benefited from the new security measures, and 2002 was without doubt the best one so far in terms of atmosphere and organisation."

We did notice one other change, which was also keenly observed by Michael Eavis, who said:

"There's certainly a sea-change going on out there right now. We're attracting a more respectful audience and that was noticeable this year. The amount of 17 and 18 year old students was grossly reduced, however you can't have the nice kids without the bad ones, so we had no choice really."

King's Meadow, at the top of the Green Fields, is a very special place with towering views across the entire festival site. It has developed great significance to many festival-goers and is known as 'Sacred Space'. In the field are the King Oak, a majestic and very old tree, a 30ft stone dragon, the peace garden and of course – the Stone Circle.

The Stone Circle is shaped to mirror the Cygnus star constellation – the swan. The stone at the tip represents the head of the swan – the bright star Albireo, which is a jewel of a double star. Under each stone are significant items that represent the direction of which each faces. There are crystals from Stonehenge, water from the Ganges, stone from the Pyramids, healing herbs and many, many other items of mystical and religious significance. While only completed in 1990 the Stone Circle feels as though it's been there forever. Here, around the Stone Circle, people gather in their hundreds with candle flares setting shadows dancing around the field, while drummers play their insistent rhythms through the night. Watching dawn break over the festival site from the Stone Circle is magical.

Dawn from the Stone Circle.

SUNDAY TICKET
Entry by bus ONLY – the bus will
you on site

security BONDED security BONDED se
BONDED security BONDED
BONDED security BON
BONDED security

2002 GLASTONBURY

Adult Child
£35/£10
Non-refundable

BUS TICKET
This portion to be retained for
return journey

From Glastonbury
Bus Stop opposite Town Hall
at 10.00hrs
Depart site at 20.00hrs

Route No
4

E 002 269

A Sunday pass is available exclusively to local residents
with the ticket guaranteeing for 2002 Rod Stewart, Roger
Waters of Pink Floyd and Isaac Hayes.

Sunday travel is provided by bus, the only way to gain
entry, to reduce congestion from various pickup points
from local towns.

GLASTONBURY 2002
28-29-30 June

– Sunday Tickets –

You've probably heard that weekend tickets for the Glastonbury Festival have all sold out. However, we would like it known that there are still **Sunday tickets** available exclusively for local residents.

This is a great opportunity for those who missed getting tickets for the whole event, people who would like a taste of the festival, or even those with camping phobia!

Says Michael Eavis: 'These Sunday tickets are a bargain unrivalled by any other event in the country – and it's on your doorstep! We're not yet revealing the full line-up, but I can disclose that Sunday performers on the legendary Pyramid Stage include **Rod Stewart**, **Roger Waters** of Pink Floyd, **Isaac Hayes** and **Jools Holland**. On the pop front, Sunday includes **Air**, **Badly Drawn Boy** and **Zero Seven**. So, book now before it's too late!'

The ticket price includes travel to and from the site on special buses from nine local towns: **Castle Cary**, **Cheddar**, **Frome**, **Glastonbury**, **Midsomer Norton**, **Radstock**, **Shepton Mallet**, **Street** and **Wells**.

We expect demand to be heavy, so book as soon as you can!

Price: Adults £35/Children £10 (covers cost of bus journey).

Booking/further info: 01749 890470.

supporting **GREENPEACE** Oxfam  **WaterAid** *and worthwhile local causes*

The Radio 1 stage as it's starting to get light.

2003

27 – 29 June

2003 would be acclaimed as the best yet with tickets selling out within 24 hours, setting a new record. The weather was perfect, the atmosphere was described as chilled and, thankfully, after the previous year's events Pilton was crime free. The line up was described as brilliant. Over a million pounds was paid to local groups and charities. Greenpeace, Oxfam and Water Aid were the main beneficiaries and on site Fairtrade led a high profile campaign.

Security was if anything tighter than the previous year with extra police and CCTV coverage. Pilton had adopted a non-alcohol zone within the village with the local pub, The Crown, shut. The message was clear:

> *"Please respect the villagers' right to live their life as normal, and with luck they'll respect the festival, getting a licence each year is made harder by the problems they suffer."*

The message was also broadcast widely *"If you don't have a ticket please stay clear you WILL NOT get in."*

Acts included: Love with Arthur Lee, Damien Rice, De la Soul, Flaming Lips, Jimmy Cliff, Moby, Radiohead, REM, The Damned, The Darkness, The Thrills, Tokyo Ska , Bill Bailey, Ross Noble and Black Sky. There was a huge variety of kids' entertainment and the creative madness that is Lost Vagueness.

The attendance increased on the previous year with 150,000 tickets made available, now £105 each including a programme. There were criticisms that the previous year's festival lacked atmosphere, because of the reduced number of people, which reflected the smaller numbers jumping the fence. Ticket sales this year were instant compared to the two months it took to sell 140,000 in 2002.

This was also the first year that tickets sold out before the full line-up was announced. Radiohead returned to headline the Pyramid Stage. The world premiere screening of *The Last Night London Burned* took place in the Left Field on Friday documenting the last live performance of ex-Clash legends Joe Strummer and Mick Jones in November 2002, before Joe's death in December that year.

The festival had a distinctive Jamaican theme running through it, helping to make the sun that did shine a little brighter for a while. Jimmy Cliff won applause for his greatest hits, remembering the old days of original reggae and The Skatalites were energetic with the earlier sounds from the island. Jazz Jamaica's repertoire was a stomping mixture of Ska and Bluebeat with everyone upon their feet. A version of Millie's *My Boy Lollypop* really got the crowd skanking.

The festival was an all round success with the number of thefts from individuals down to around 60 and reported theft from tents down to around 130. Michael Eavis said he was delighted with the drop in crime, adding:

"Last night was the first night ever when I haven't had a phone call in the night from some irate neighbour."

The 2003 Jamaican theme starred singer, song-writer and actor Jimmy Cliff.

Opposite: Guns of Navarone: The Skatalites from Jamaica featuring Lester Sterling.

The 2003 line-up was varied, heralded brilliant, and included Manic Street Preachers and Thom Yorke of Radiohead.

2004

25 – 27 June

The Other stage and a deep blue

"A massive over-demand for tickets frustrated all concerned. The weather in the run up to the festival was not on our side. However, the improved drainage and organisation triumphed to contribute to the safest ever festival. Working together for a greener Glastonbury paid off, with 32% of all waste recycled, including 110 tons of organic waste composted. Streams and hedges remained unpolluted, she-pees were installed. Coffee and chocolate were Fairtrade. On top of the £1,000,000 paid to Greenpeace, Water Aid, Oxfam and local good causes, an additional £100,000 was donated to the Sudan appeal. This was the year of The Tower – a massive 70 ft tall moving structure erected adjacent to Left Field to celebrate working together. The Unsigned Performer's Competition was launched. The Pyramid stage had its normal eclectic range of performances, including English National Opera playing to an audience of 15,000 and a larger crowd watching England play (estimate 65,000) than actually attended the World Cup Stadium in person."

Acts included: Paul McCartney, Muse, Oasis, James Brown, Joss Stone, Toots and The Maytals, Franz Ferdinand, Scissor Sisters, Black Eyed Peas, Sister Sledge, Television, Michael Franti and Spearhead. The Green Fields and particularly Lost Vagueness were a mass of innovative, creative and amazing sights and sounds. Over 1200 acts in The Cabaret, Theatre and Circus Fields included The Generating Company, Helios – The Saga of a 1000 Suns and Albatross while the Kidz Field was a profusion of fun and colour, workshops and parades.

Sir Paul McCartney

Sir Paul McCartney announced on the Saturday night, *"It's great to finally be here in Glastonbury"* then embarked on a two and a half hour set, a mix of Beatles, Wings and Paul McCartney. The set list included *Penny Lane, Lady Madonna*, and *Yellow Submarine*. He had to endure a certain amount of heckling from some of the younger members of the crowd but before the night had ended the crowd were dancing in their wellies with *Hey Jude* inspiring one of the greatest camp fire sing-songs.

What is love? It is that powerful attraction towards all that we conceive, or fear, or hope beyond ourselves.

–Percy Bysshe Shelley

Tickets on sale from **9am, Sunday 3rd April**

Ticket price **£125** plus **£4** booking fee, plus postage

By phone – debit cards, POs and cheques only:
0870 165 2005

Online – debit cards only **www.aloud.com**

For information on what you will need to buy a ticket, call the ticketline before April 3rd, or log on to **www.glastonburyfestivals.co.uk**

2005

24 – 26 June

Glastonburyfestivals.co.uk reported:

"Lightning strikes!!! Two months worth of rain in several hours! A once in a hundred year occurrence! For those unfortunate enough to get swamped, Welfare were there to give a helping hand. All in all, everyone pulled through – dinghy's n 'all – and thoroughly enjoyed themselves whatever the weather. Sure enough the sun came out to greet us by Sunday turning it into the happiest festival yet.

The huge success of the Make Poverty History campaign was echoed at the festival, with Michael Eavis making a very rare appearance on the Pyramid stage with Bob Geldof. Greenpeace, Oxfam and Water Aid worked together declaring ...this year, let's make poverty history and clean energy our future... A remarkable £1,350,000 was paid to charities and good causes. Tickets sold out in less than three hours and 50% of all waste was recycled!

We said farewell to the Dance Tent and welcomed the new, vibrant, colourful Dance Village with eight different venues, all playing different types of dance music – including the Silent Disco. The Midnight Cabaret and The Ghost Train in the Circus Field were new fun additions that had everyone talking, along with all the fantastic sculptures around the site.

The New Tent was re-launched as the John Peel stage, in memory of all this late, great, supporter of the festival did to promote emerging talent. The Unsigned Performers Competition generated thousands of entrants, with over thirty-five acts performing in various venues, including the new, Rockin' Late 'n Live marquee in the markets."

Opposite: *Flags at the Dance Village.*

Steve Harley, a regular visitor to the festival.

The 153,000 attendees were rewarded with acts including: Steve Harley and Cockney Rebel, K.T. Tunstall, Basement Jaxx, White Stripes, Magic Numbers, Coldplay, Razorlight, New Order, Brian Wilson, James Blunt, Beautiful South, Babyshambles, The Killers, Kaiser Chiefs, The Subways, Chas n' Dave, Elvis Costello & Royksopp.

The Silent Disco was introduced by Emily Eavis allowing revellers to party into the early hours without disturbing the locals, now a requirement of the festival's licensing. Rather than the conventional speakers, music is broadcast via an FM transmitter picked up on wireless headphones, a bizarre sight if you are not wearing any as it all you see is a room full of people dancing to nothing.

The huge success of the Make Poverty History campaign was echoed at the festival, with Michael Eavis making a very rare appearance on the Pyramid stage with Bob Geldof.

John Peel Stage

This stage entered the world with the name the New Bands Tent aka New Bands, which was confusing for some as it was the tent that was new and not the bands. The one person who was not confused about this was John Peel who reportedly enjoyed its mix of new names and old names. For this reason when the festival's dear friend departed this world in 2004 it was universally decided to honour the festival by using his name for this stage.

John Peel was one of the first broadcasters to play progressive rock on British radio and was widely acknowledged for promoting amongst other genres; alternative rock, punk and reggae. His Radio One shows were legendary in promoting new bands and his 'Peel Sessions', consisting of three or four songs recorded live at the BBC, often gave artists their first airing on national radio. One such band in 1973 featured a young Jamaican by the name of Bob Marley along with Peter Tosh and The Wailers who like many went on to achieve worldwide fame.

It was not uncommon for an artist who had appeared on John's show to crop up at the Pilton site on one of the smaller stages, Pulp and David Bowie were both championed by John during their formative years, both later becoming headliners at the festival.

Perhaps the most appropriate tribute to John's Glastonbury legacy came from Michael Eavis, who re-named the New Bands stage the John Peel stage. Michael said:

"It's very appropriate because it's all the sort of music that John would have chosen."

John Peel made a massive contribution to the Glastonbury experience, whether he was introducing bands, being spotted wandering through the site or sitting on a hay bale looking at the wrong camera. John didn't manage to get to every Glastonbury Festival over the years but his broadcasts on both radio and television have come to symbolise the spirit of the ever-eclectic event.

2007

22 – 24 June

Glastonburyfestivals.co.uk recorded:

"2007 may have been another year of mud and rain, but it was nothing that Glastonbury Festival-goers couldn't handle, thanks to a strong line up, continually improving drainage and an indomitable collective will to enjoy, that held off the worst effects of the wet and mud like a matching rainbow umbrella and welly set.

The worthwhile causes supported by the festival joined forces for the I Count campaign, which highlighted the need to address climate change, and signed up 70,000 people to the campaign over the weekend, an impressive 46% of all 153,000 ticket holders on site. Glastonbury 2007 also strove to be the greenest one so far, with Bags For Life given out and festival-goers encouraged not to bring loo rolls as recycled ones were provided at the festival.

This year saw the introduction of Emily Eavis' Park stage, bringing a whole new section of the festival site to life, whilst the Dance Village cemented its reputation in its second year. The Unsigned Bands Competition became the Emerging Talent Competition, which again generated thousands of entries and a host of worthy winners playing on many of the festival stages. Also introduced this year was the award winning anti-touting registration system for ticket buyers.

The Arctic Monkeys played their first Glastonbury set headlining the Pyramid stage on the Friday night and The Who pulled out all the stops as the closing band on Sunday. Other acts to play included Bjork, Shirley Bassey, Iggy Pop, CSS, The Go Team, Amy Winehouse, MIA, Kate Nash, Billy Bragg (it wouldn't feel like Glastonbury without him), Corinne Bailey Rae, Damian Marley, Lily Allen and The Chemical Brothers.

Attendance: 135,000 weekend tickets, 37,500 passes (for crew, performers, stewards, traders, etc and 5000 Sunday tickets. Tickets were £145 including programme".

Piney Gir

Piney grew up in virtual isolation in the American Midwest; she went to a special Christian school (no Darwin, no sex education) and attended church 4-5 times a week (no sinful TV, no secular music). This left a lot to young Piney's imagination which flourished to fill in all the gaps... Playing music from the age of four and writing songs in her bedroom from the age of nine, Piney went on to university to study percussion, but her shabby, ghetto apartment was robbed and they took her drums. So she changed her major to voice; "They can't steal your voice!" she reckoned. However, Piney never had the voice for Verdi and eventually came to London to work in a cocktail bar, go to art school for a bit and figure things out.

She joined her first band, a synth pop duo (Vic Twenty) who released a single on Mute and toured Europe with Erasure. After seeing the world, she realised the road was in her blood, music was her sense of purpose and so she released her debut album *Peakahokahoo* on Truck Records in 2004. This was followed by singles and EP's released with all-girl, art-rock, cult-classic group The Schla La Las. Whilst touring she decided to try playing country versions of her songs. This led to the formation of The Piney Gir Country Roadshow, and a release of country album Hold Yer Horses. The album contains new versions of songs previously released on *Peakahokahoo*. *Hold Yer Horses* was selected as one of the top five albums of 2006 by Phill Jupitus in his music column for the *Radio Times* magazine, stating that "the stomp and twang of these songs of love and life are unmissable."

Piney Gir with Ian Kellett on banjo.

She then went on to release *The Yearling* on Hotel Records in 2009; Damaged Goods picked her up for The Piney Gir Country Roadshow's 2nd album *Jesus Wept* in 2010 and the Piney Gir album *Geronimo!* in 2011.

The review in the *Guardian* was written by Jude Rogers:

Stage: the Park

Dress code: Surely the most fabulous frock Glastonbury has given us so far – a rootin', tootin', square-dancing dress, with a skirt so full of frothy white netting that your grandmother's window will surely be unbeaten tonight.

In summary: Forty minutes of skirt-swinging fun from Kansas City born, London living Piney Gir – full of music that should turn the sky blue and puts the sun in your heart. Metaphorically, it does this in spades; every accordion-squeezing, banjo-twanging hoedown being an utter delight.

Highlight: A wonderful soft country reading of Bruce Springsteen's Dancing in the Dark, complete with backing vocals and sultry squeezebox.

Lowlight: The dank, unremitting rain.

Unusual occurrences: A thirty-second spate of sunlight as the set closer, Greetings Salutations Goodbye, winds its merry way to a close

Opposite: *The Pyramid stage and a small amount of sunshine.*

2008

27 – 29 June

Here comes the sun … after a little rain

The past two festivals were blighted by rain and mud but this year Mother Nature was kind with a smidgen of the wet stuff, sufficient to keep the dust at bay, with the fabulous music and entertainment topped off by the fine weather. It was another sell out, albeit slower than other years, but that had to be expected given the inclement condition of the two previous extravaganzas. The charitable donations continued as in previous years with admission price now set at £155 and the crowd limit set at 134,000 including the allocation of 6000 Sunday tickets.

Controversy surrounded the headline act Jay-Z, the rap star, with many suggesting that rap had no place at Glastonbury. The theory was disproved with a storming show that drew a substantial passionate crowd. This was a year of electrifying sets with golden oldies interspersed with emerging talent with Solomon Burke, Joan Baez, Gilbert O'Sullivan, Jimmy Cliff, Joan Armatrading, and Neil Diamond going down a storm. But it would be Leonard Cohen who led the crowd in an astonishing chorus of 'Hallelujah', performing his greatest hits as the sun went down on the festival's final day. Others notable contributors were Manu Chao, Massive Attack, Groove Armada, Seasick Steve, Lupe Fiasco, Mark Ronson, Dizzee Rascal, Ozomatli , Eddy Grant, Stanton Warriors, Natty, Dr Meaker, Fun Loving Criminals, The National, Tunng and Laura Marling. Katie Melua and Will Young gave intimate sets at the Avalon stage. The Park continued to grow from strength to strength, and Trash City, in its new home, and Shangrli-la kept festival goers dancing 'til dawn.

Arabella Churchill

This years was overshadowed by the passing away of Arabella Churchill in December 2007. Arabella Churchill was the granddaughter of Winston Churchill, British Prime Minister during the war years, and was one of the key figures of the Glastonbury Festival. It was late 1970 after the first Fayre had taken place that she arrived at Worthy Farm with Andrew Kerr and friends who were described affectionately as upper-crust hippies. Her vision was to hold a free festival at the farm to coincide with the summer solstice. Arabella continued as one of the most valuable members of the team at Worthy Farm, and from 1981 she was solely responsible for the development and running of the Theatre and Circus Fields at the festival.

The front of a plane
in Shangri-la

In keeping with her Buddhist faith, a simple farewell to Arabella Churchill took place on the final evening of the festival. Michael Eavis paid this tribute after her death, *"Her energy, vitality and great sense of morality and social responsibility have given her a place in our festival history second to none."* In 2010 Michael received a donation from British Waterways of timber taken from the old gates at Caen Hill Lock near Devizes in Wiltshire. This would be used to construct a new bridge dedicated to her memory at the festival site called Bella's Bridge, crossing the Whitelake River.

The Theatre and Circus Fields are set away from the main stages. The fields are located on some of the most historic and beautiful farmland in Somerset, along the eastern fringes of the site.

Opposite: *Manu Chao closing the Jazz World stage.*

2009

24 – 28 June

Last year's festival was seen as a triumph over adversity and tickets were sold out for the 2009 festival before the end of April. A record number of festival-goers had already set up camp on the Thursday morning with estimates suggesting over 90,000 had already gained entry to the site. The crowds were eager with anticipation despite weather forecasters predicting a deluge to hit the rolling Mendip Hills, and on cue the skies above the Vale of Avalon darkened and the torrential rain arrived. The festival web site described the next few hours:

> "Thursday evening saw the day's clear sky darken with some ominous-looking storm clouds. Lightning strobe-lit the valley and a torrential downpour did its best to drench fairy wings and dampen spirits. But umbrellas were opened and spirits remained impenetrable. The clouds moved on for good, leaving only some muddy puddles and smug welly wearers in their wake."

The untimely death of Michael Jackson swept through the crowd and many accolades to his music were heard throughout the weekend from his fellow artists including Lily Allen back on the Pyramid stage wearing one white glove.

Kasabian playing the Pyramid stage.
One of the biggest crowds of the weekend.

The festival website continued:

"Despite Jackson's death, the mood on site remained up-beat. On Friday morning, Abba parody Björn Again opened the Pyramid stage, and from that point, the performance highlights came thick and fast. Fleet Foxes' sweet harmonies serenaded a sun-dappled afternoon throng; Little Boots and Lady Gaga dazzled; Ray Davies and Neil Young delivered classic sets.

Rolf Harris' Saturday performance jammed the Jazz/World stage; Dizzee Rascal marked his arrival as a bona fide star at the Pyramid; Florence and the Machine rocked a rammed John Peel Tent and the frenzied excitement that consumed the crowd watching Pendulum on the Other stage was only surpassed by those cheering on The Boss as he broke into Born To Run *in his headline set on the Pyramid.*

Sunday's sing-a-longs came courtesy of golden oldies Tom Jones and Tony Christie. Nick Cave's tremulous sun-down set was upstaged by a plucky – though unsuccessful – would-be gatecrasher attempting to defy the fence by flying in via microlite, while later; The Prodigy tore up the Other stage. But it was hard to top a reunited Blur's return to Glastonbury. Hailed as the best Pyramid set in an age, the unfaltering show and its ecstatic reception even moved Damon Albarn to tears. Emotional and elated, he wasn't alone."

Michael hailed 2009 as *"the best Glastonbury ever"* a sentiment repeated many times before but nonetheless still true with 135,000 paying £175 each for a weekend ticket with a further 5000 Sunday tickets snapped up.

Lily Allen wearing 'one white glove'.

Joe Strummer – Strummerville

Bruce Springsteen closed the second night of the festival paying tribute to the late Clash front-man Joe Strummer. Springsteen's headlining show on the Pyramid stage, his first ever festival appearance in Britain, was one of the most anticipated of the weekend. Springsteen, a huge Clash and Strummer fan, chose to open the set with a solo rendition of Strummer's track *Coma Girl* a track originally recorded with The Mescaleros. The song's lyrics were inspired by the Festival, with Joe Strummer a regular visitor up until his death in 2002. A visibly moved Springsteen is reported to have told a packed crowd: *"We're so pleased to be here at the rain-free Glastonbury! I've heard about it. I've heard about it! And now I can see it. The E Street Band are here to honour the solemn vow to rock the house tonight!"*

Joe Strummer will be immortalised within rock'n'roll history. He channelled attitude and purpose with great punk-rock anthems to become a voice of a generation. His words and The Clash's music still influence a generation of young musicians who want to make music with something to say rather than just be one of the crowd. The charity Strummerville aims to maintain this legacy, allowing young musicians with the opportunity to play gigs, get their music heard, and help share the spirit of Joe for years to come. Think what Joe Strummer would have done. This is probably pretty good advice when discovering what Strummerville is all about. The charity hopes to retain the ethos, charisma and ethics of Joe and keep them going for all to enjoy.

Strummerville was set up after Joe's death in 2002, by family and friends, to cement the views that Joe believed in, and to make sure as many people as possible have the chance to learn something from the man in the years to come. After all, everybody has a story to tell. The man who would go on to have huge record sales started off as a busker with little idea about how to write songs, let alone how to record them. Fuelled by just a record collection, a guitar and passionate view on life, Joe and The Clash would become one the figureheads of the emerging '70s punk scene. Strummerville aims to make it easier for musicians to share their music with others, get access to recording studios while at the same time teaching bands to stand on their own two feet. A DIY, punk ethic which can be stretched across a wide range of musical genres.

He was the political edge of the band as they strove towards writing intelligent and enthralling pop-punk songs. This is something that stays with Strummerville today, championing bands that have something important, interesting or enlightening to say. Within this though, there is a lot of fun in the music with the aim being to create invigorating songs that bring people together.

The Campfire sessions have continued the legacy of Joe's campfire community at Glastonbury where people can come to drink, talk and laugh with some like-minded individuals, and some good music. Set in the place where Joe held his annual campfire, 2008 saw the likes of Frank Turner and The Drums perform intimate sets for a lucky crowd of gatherers.

Strummerville is excited to have a host of amazing artists grace their tiny stage by the campfire. The Strummerville notice reads: "No bands are announced in advance, so drop by and see who is on our chalk board each day."

Strummerville believes in helping all styles of music develop. It is about artists organically finding their feet. The charity helps to sow the seeds and then waits to see what grows.

Joe Strummer had his campfire here for years – he always hosted a huge campfire at the festival. After he passed away and the family set up the charity Michael Eavis put an amazing memory stone in place for him. The campfire burns by the memory stone. He died in 2002 and in 2003 the charity began running the campfire.

The pre-festival notes read:

> *In our usual spot by the Joe Strummer memory stone in the Unfair Ground, Strummerville will be burning our traditional campfire all weekend long, bringing good vibes, great music and lots of love... We will be presenting some new talent and will be joined by some friends for some special intimate campfire sessions.*
>
> *Everyone is welcome.*

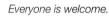

The Ribbon Tower in the Park at sunset and
(right) The Streets on the Jazz World stage.

2010 – 40th Anniversary

25 – 27 June

Glastonbury celebrated its 40th anniversary in 2010, a milestone that brought a fresh buzz of excitement to the Worthy Farm valley. The weather was also suitably celebratory, with warm days and balmy starlit nights. Car parks opened up on the Tuesday night for the first time prior to the pedestrian gates opening on the Wednesday morning. From 2100 on Tuesday night to around midnight, vehicles flowed into car parks with no problems. From 0600 traffic levels increased dramatically with major queues developing on all routes by 0730 as many people tried to arrive for the 0800 pedestrian gate opening. Between 0800 and 1400 there were delays on all routes to the site with the longest being on the route from the M5. The vast majority of ticket holders arrived on site on the Wednesday, earlier than in any previous year.

With the sun beating down relentlessly the demand for water was enormous, so the decision to build a second new permanent reservoir this year was more than vindicated. Both reservoirs hold about a million litres of drinking water each. Just over 800 taps were installed across the site as well as 600 basins, but there were still queues for water. In 2010, there were also some 4600 toilets (a mix of long-drops, African, polyjohns and flushing) and 670 metres of urinals for the guys and a much more modest 100 metres of 'she pees' for women. Visually, the anniversary was recognised by two giant dates on either side of the Pyramid stage and a Hollywood-style display of letters that spelled out Glastonbury 40 across the site's southern grassy slopes. Classic photos taken by local Somerset photographers across the decades were exhibited in the main backstage area. Several performers from the original 1970 event appeared, including DJ Mad Mick, who dropped the festival's very first tune. The Left Field stage returned in a different position (close to the Glade) and with a new curator, Billy Bragg. More music was mixed with the usual wide range of political discussion and debate. For the second year running a giant screen of painted and embroidered banners broadcast messages such as 'Give Bees a Chance'. Two new areas were created in the late night corner of the festival – the Common and the Unfair Ground. Arcadia shot bursts of fire into the sky from its temple-like structures as dance music pumped through the night. Shangri-la's casaba of the weird and wonderful was as rammed as ever.

A new bridge flanked with local Mendip stone was erected over the Whitelake stream and named Bella's Bridge after Theatre Fields founder Arabella Churchill, who died in 2007. This year's Theatre and Circus highlights included Colombia's Circo Para Todos, the Russian troupe BlackSkyWhite and slack-rope walker Kwabana Lindsay cutting a hornpipe between the tent tops. The Jazz World stage was given a new identity as West Holts. This was the original name of a 'halt' on the railway line which once ran through Worthy Farm; Michael Eavis said:

"I could remember driving cattle across it before the next train arrived."

Opposite: *Thom Yorke in the Park.*

Sunday was given a downside by the defeat of England's footballers in the World Cup, an event for which two special fields were allocated with their own giant screens. 80,000 fans watched the match. More successful was a game played out in front of the Pyramid stage on Thursday, when festival-goers representing England beat the rest of the World and raised £9000 for charity.

As ever, there were many musical highlights. Gorillaz filled the Friday night Pyramid headline slot with grooves and guests, following U2's enforced cancellation, although the band's guitarist, The Edge, did turn up to do a song with Muse for their storming Saturday night slot. The final headliner, Stevie Wonder, brought things to a close on Sunday night with a wonderful, hit-filled set, which memorably also featured a duet of Happy Birthday with Michael Eavis.

Aside from the headliners, Shakira and Scissor Sisters lit up the Pyramid stage on Saturday with suitably exuberant pop (the latter featured a guest performance from Kylie Minogue), while Biffy Clyro and Radiohead's Thom Yorke/Jonny Greenwood played warmly-received surprise slots in the Park. Other Stage highlights included a rousing Pet Shop Boys set, a huge turnout for Florence and The Machine and a guest appearance from Doctor Who for Orbital's Sunday night set. Meanwhile, at the John Peel stage, Groove Armada, Mumford & Sons and The XX were among the acts that attracted big crowds and warm reviews. Over in the Dance Village, Glastonbury veterans The Orb and Fatboy Slim once again whipped up a storm, while the rise in urban pop music was reflected with blistering sets from acts including N-Dubz, Chipmunk, Plan B, Kelis and Tinie Tempah.

It was, all would agree, a vintage year. Michael Eavis told the world's media at his traditional Sunday morning press conference:

> "It has been the best party for me – the weather, the full moon and last night a crowd of 100,000 people, every single one enjoying themselves."

Attendance: 135,000 weekend tickets, 37,500 passes (for crew, performers, stewards, traders etc,) and 5000 Sunday tickets. Ticket price was £185

The Green Fields are the soul of Glastonbury Festival where traditional skills and new ways of thinking combine in an explosion of creativity. They occupy the highest ground at the top end of the site, overlooking the rest of the festival, and keeping watch over its basic principles. This enchanting area still encapsulates the spirit and ideals which inspired the very first Pilton festivals. With its skyline filled with peace flags, gently turning wind generators and the outlines of dozens of tipis, this is a place to discover that there are other ways to make the world turn round other than competing and consuming.

The fox at Avalon.

The Green Fields are about change and discovery – learning how to release your own potential, and discovering how to change the world. The Green movement encompasses both, from the small ways in which we can change our personal lifestyle, to the big challenges of shifting the direction of international politics. The Green Fields are about doing things for ourselves, but at the same time doing them in a way that is communal, inclusive and caring.

The Green Fields are also fun. So you can pedal yourself into a mild sweat making sure the batteries for the PA keep charged, relax with a soothing massage session, listen to bands in a solar-powered marquee, or join in a heated discussion about the best ways to cool the planet or learn how to bake your own bread in an open air oven. This is the place to escape the frenetic activity of the rest of the festival, to relax and maybe to meditate. There are endless ways in which you can open up your mind and your body.

The path from West Holts to the Green Fields.

2011

24 – 26 June
Sunshine and showers

Tickets for the festival went on sale from nine am on Sunday 3 October 2010 with the cost now £195 plus £5 booking fee. All tickets were sold out in four hours. Several thousand revellers packed the site early, many arriving with still two days to go. Last year's festival was a scorching success including the weather but the skies above Pilton were laden with rain. Notwithstanding, over 175,000 were determined to enjoy the weekend as they would have to wait another two years for the next, the farm taking a breather to allow the grass to recover much like it had done in 2001 and 2006.

Official attendance figures: 135,000 weekend, 37,500 passes and 5000 Sunday tickets. Over £2 million was raised for Water Aid, Greenpeace, Oxfam as well as other local good causes. Since 2000 each year the festival has paid over £1m to charities and local good causes in Pilton and the local community and include:

*The completion of a housing project providing 22 houses with afford-
   able rent for offspring of villagers who cannot afford Pilton prices.
Renovating the Glastonbury Abbey Tithe Barn in Pilton and establish-
   ing the Pilton Barn Trust.
Building the original pavilion, football pitch, tennis courts in Pilton Play-
   ing Fields.
Building the new Pilton Working Men's Club.
Rebuilding of the Pilton Playing Fields Pavilion.
Renovation of the child's play area in the Pilton Playing Fields.
Recasting the damaged medieval bells in Pilton parish church.
Repairing the Pilton parish church heating system.
Providing and erecting stone squeeze styles for footpaths in Pilton.
Repairing the Pilton Methodist chapel roof.
Improving the fabric and facilities of Glastonbury library.*

BB King took his seat on the Pyramid stage and launched into 'Everyday I Have The Blues', The legendary 85 year old proved he is king of the Blues.

The figures provided by the Economic Impact Survey jointly funded by Mendip District Council and Glastonbury Festival, carried out by an independent consultancy, indicate that the net value of the 2007 Festival to the Mendip economy was over £35m and for the West Country over £100m.

For the past twenty-years Michael Eavis has arranged the Pilton Party, attracting top acts seeking a spot at the following year's Festival. Villagers run the bar with all proceeds from the event going to the village show and to other village ventures. In 2007 the Pilton Party generated some £15,000 for the Village Show committee, and £30,000 for the Village Hall.

Back to the festival, and the rain was trying its best to dampen the spirits of all, but on Friday night on the Pyramid stage Bono and his band tore through a powerful, career-spanning set, while later Morrissey and BB King kept the crowds' spirits high. Saturday highlights on the Pyramid included Coldplay, Paolo Nutini, whilst Sunday witnessed the stage opening with the stirring baritones of Port Isaac's Fisherman's Friends, Beyoncé and Paul Simon resurrecting his past hits. As the evening drew in pastel skies prevailed as the sun set on another great year.

In their review of the weekend, virtualfestivals.com wrote enthusiatically:

> Maybe it's because there's a fallow year a-comin' but Glastonbury 2011 packs in more surprises than a Kinder Egg factory.

> Take the weather for starters; there's biblical rain on Thursday, the type of downpour that has campers awake but sat with their tents firmly zipped up. Noah's Ark doesn't bob by like it did in 2005, but it's enough for mud-diving revellers and a host of floating wreckage down by the John Peel tent. Then come Sunday, it's the hottest Glastonbury day in five years and the only ones without sunburn are the bloody Wombles who stay hidden in their enormous furry costumes.

> Thanks to a spat with Mikey E, the group have thousands crammed into the Avalon Stage too, for a show that's ironically rubbish. The whole thing smacks of PR guff. Radiohead create their own stink with an unannounced set on the Park stage where much of 'The King Of Limbs' gets a scruffy airing. A few In Rainbows numbers fare best, in particular Arpeggi, but on the whole it's a bit deflating.

> If they need help, they could share a chair with Pulp whose vintage surprise gig shows maturity and energy in abundance. Reaching his twilight years, Jarvis Cocker may banter like an elder gentleman between songs but he still knows how to wiggle along to brilliant workings of Sorted For Es and Whizz and Common People.

Crowds turn up to see Pulp.

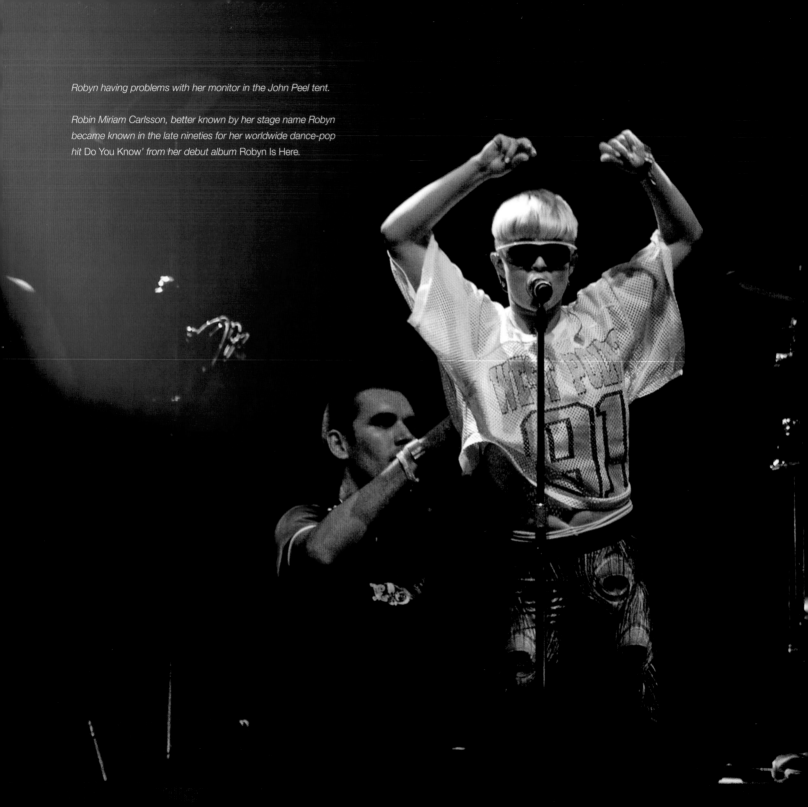

Robyn having problems with her monitor in the John Peel tent.

Robin Miriam Carlsson, better known by her stage name Robyn became known in the late nineties for her worldwide dance-pop hit Do You Know' from her debut album Robyn Is Here.

Beyonce adds a little glamour to proceedings with a glitzy headline show. She kicks off with what could be a sparkling finale: a barnstorming *Crazy In Love* and a roar of fireworks.

Single Ladies (Put A Ring On It) and *Naughty Girl* follow with a cameo from Tricky, who doesn't seem to do much except look like a rabbit blinded by headlights. It's the awful run of ballads from her new offering 4 that slows proceedings, but a medley of *Destiny's Child* numbers and a smooth Etta James cover closes the curtain in triumphant theatrical style.

Stadium rockers U2 and Coldplay are one and the same: astute and professional with true headline pedigree. The former feel a little needy wanting to be liked but it's an outstanding career-spanning dam-buster, while Chris Martin goes chocolate tongued, reworking the lyrics to *What A Wonderful World* to fit with Glastonbury which had "the greatest audience you'll ever hear". That aside the band are stunning.

Elsewhere, Wu-Tang Clan ease into Saturday afternoon with plenty of swagger and chunky hip hop tracks and Tinie Tempah shows that UK rappers can rule the Pyramid stage too with an energetic, hit-packed set. Mumford And Sons cap their fourth successive Glasto with a charming performance on the Other stage. They play four new songs among the *Sigh No More* favourites and if they're an indication of where they're headed, what price for them to headline in 2013? Elbow, who is equally as special, might beat them to it. Looking significantly overwhelmed, Guy Garvey leads his band mates through a set that ticks all the prerequisite boxes for a sunset slot on the Pyramid stage: backing from a mini orchestra, crowd participation, massive sing-along and bizarre chat about phantom poos.

One final surprise Glastonbury 2011 has up its wizard sleeve is a sublime showing from Wild Beasts, It's hairs on the back of the neck time with a blissed-out selection of *Smother* tracks and the type of quality found only for the most masterful musicians.

Now it's time to head to Shangri-La before people start queuing in the one-way system for 2013.

Jimmy Cliff.

Jimmy Cliff

Jimmy Cliff (James Chambers) was born on 1 April 1948 in the Somerton district of St James, Jamaica. He began writing songs from an early age whilst still at primary school. Moving to the capital in 1962 he sought out producers whilst he was still at Kingston Technical School, always trying but without success to get his songs recorded.

He entered many talent contests but his first break came when he met Leslie Kong and they decided to get into the music business. It was his third single that launched him onto the music scene in Jamaica with *Hurricane Hattie*, a single that became a huge hit for Jimmy in Jamaica at the tender age of 14.

1972 saw Jimmy Cliff become a truly international star playing Ivanhoe 'Ivan' Martin in the film *The Harder They Come*. Directed by the late Perry Henzell the film tells the story of a young man drawn to the ghettos of Kingston from the country by the promise of making it in the record business. Success eludes him and he inevitably turns to a life of crime. The soundtrack elevated reggae to the world stage and still remains one of the most significant works to have come out of Jamaica.

In May 2009 Paolo Nutini *(above)* released *Sunny Side Up*, his second album that debuted at number one in the UK and produced four hit singles, including *Coming Up Easy, Pencil Full Of Lead* and *10/10*.

Giselle Knowles-Carter better known by her stage name Beyoncé.

2013

26 – 30 June

Tickets went on sale at 9am on Sunday 7 October 2012 and were soon snapped up. A message announcing the sell-out was made.

After one hour and forty minutes, tickets for Glastonbury 2013 have now completely sold out (in record time). We would like to say an enormous thanks to everyone who managed to buy a ticket – but we'd also like to extend our sincere apologies to the many thousands who missed out.

We're genuinely humbled by the sheer number of people who would like to come to the festival, and we dearly wish we could have you all along. Sadly, that just isn't possible, which means a significant number of people have missed out. Tickets were being sold through the morning – but demand simply outstripped supply.

If you were one of those who managed to get a ticket, then we look forward to welcoming you to Worthy Farm in June. If not then there is likely to be a resale of returned tickets in the spring, and your registration will also remain valid for future Glastonbury Festivals – so we hope to see you down here at some point.

Thank you all again for your incredible support for Glastonbury Festival.

Michael and Emily Eavis.

Here we are forty-three years on from the first festival at Worthy Farm. How time's winged chariot has moved on – a remarkable achievement celebrating over four decades of Glastonbury Festival. Michael wrote in his foreword to this book, how long will the Glastonbury ticket remain magical? I suspect as many do for a good while yet: what a milestone it would be to reach fifty.

Back to today and the time of year when the enchanted city appears, merely for a fleeting moment in time, deep within the heart of the Somerset countryside. The ticket price for 2013 has now reached £205 plus a booking and postage fee of £11. One of the headline acts, The Rolling Stones, made a rare festival appearance on Saturday night, their only other of note in two decades being the Isle of Wight Festival back in 2007.

Festival goers began queuing on Tuesday night and by Friday 175,000 were on site. Michael praised the weather and festival plans: "The whole thing is fantastic, there are 1000 acres of creativity on a massive scale and to a very, very high standard, you won't see anything else like this in the whole world." Michael describing the situation surrounding the coverage of The Stones' set by the BBC said, "It's taken a long time to get them to come and play, everyone wants to see The Stones, basically I think Mick Jagger wanted to play to the people here, rather than a TV show." The Pyramid stage area has been extended this year allowing the tens of thousands of fans enjoying the set to avoid any problems with overcrowding.

The Pyramid stage featured on Friday: Arctic Monkeys, Dizzee Rascal, The Vaccines, Professor Green, Rita Ora, Jake Bugg and Haim. Toumani Diabaté was forced to withdraw from his opening slot due to illness and was replaced by Jupiter and Okwess International.

Saturday: The Rolling Stones, Primal Scream, Elvis Costello, Ben Howard, Laura Mvula, Billy Bragg and RokiaTraoré.

Sunday: Mumford and Sons, Nick Cave and the Bad Seeds, Vampire Weekend, Kenny Rogers, Rufus Wainwright, First Aid Kit and Bassekou Kouyate.

Saturday: It's been a long time since the Pyramid stage saw a crowd of the size gathered for The Rolling Stones. Quite possibly it's not been this busy here since the night when The Levellers played to a rammed field the year the fence came down and the whole site groaned under the weight of extra numbers.

Bursting with energy that belies their years The Stones start as they mean to go on – with an exuberant flourish. *Jumping Jack Flash* and *Only Rock'n'Roll* kick off a two-and-a-half hour marathon at a blistering sprint, and Jagger's swagger never leaving him throughout the show. "They finally got round to asking us," grins the stick-thin soon-to-be-septuagenarian, knowing full well that getting the band to play has been an ambition of Michael Eavis' for probably as long as the festival has been going. But apart from the odd one-liner the patter between songs is kept to a minimum so the band could plunder the deepest corners of their back-catalogue. Amongst the more obvious and to-be-expected numbers (*Honky Tonk Woman* and *Paint It, Black* being a couple of fine examples), the band took the opportunity to throw in a few more esoteric tracks, along with last year's single, *Doom And Gloom*.

Two Thousand Light Years From Home is sprung as a psychedelic surprise, and another treat for the night is the return of Mick Taylor, Ronnie Wood's predecessor in the band, who guests on *Can't You Hear Me Knocking* and *Midnight Rambler*, a great song that gives Sir Mick a chance to show off his harmonica skills to full effect. Sadly the much-anticipated flaming animatronics phoenix sitting poised and waiting atop the Pyramid stage all weekend is something of an anticlimax, more detracting from the otherwise excellent *Sympathy For The Devil* than adding anything special to the moment.

A two-song encore followed a nervous minute or so where worried fans wondered whether that was it after Mick and Co rather abruptly left the stage as the closing notes of *Brown Sugar* still echoed across the field. Joined by the London Youth Choir and the Voce Chamber Choir for *You Can't Always Get What You Want* and rounding off perhaps predictably (but who'd have wanted it any other way?) with *(I Can't Get No) Satisfaction* – complete with giant confetti canons and fireworks – the feeling is that yes, it may have taken all these years for The Stones to finally appear at Glastonbury, but it was worth the wait.

Sunday: There was an atmosphere of excitement and anticipation before Mumford and Sons' Sunday night headline appearance at the Pyramid stage. Were they really ready for this enormous responsibility? To fill the muddy boots of the Springsteens and Wonders and REMs of old? Sure, it's been a hectic rise for the West London band. It's only been a few years since we first spotted them half way up the Far Out stage at Green Man. It was certainly welcome to witness an actual folk band headline this festival which has acoustic guitars and earthly tales running down its ley lines like the pulped apples that run through the delicious toxic potions from the Cider Bus.

What follows is a spiralling, heady waltz of a set, Mumford and Sons turning the Pyramid field into one gigantic barn dance. *Holland*

Road takes us by our hand and spins us around, and *Babel* moves from a gentle sensual sway into a fiery, incendiary jig.

The Pyramid field is clearly emptier than Saturday's triumphant Rolling Stones performance, but this is an equally memorable gig. They've been staying at Worthy Farm for the last three days, they tell the crowd half way through the set, and this is their fifth appearance here. Glastonbury veterans then, for a band still so young this really is impressive. "We feel we didn't do anything special to get here. But we're proud to be here. And we're glad you got us here," Marcus says before they close with a beautiful, endearing *Awake My Soul* and bring The Vaccines, The Staves and Vampire Weekend out to help them with a raucous cover of *With A Little Help From My Friends*. They're humble words, and it's clear that this is just the first of future Glastonbury memories.

The festival web site posted the following message on the Monday:

Thank you all for making it a truly vintage year for Glastonbury. It really was one of the best.
Michael and Emily.

As the sun set on a wonderful 2013 festival let's take a fleeting look back to 1970 to remember just how significantly the festival has grown. Keith Christmas, one of the first performers, who incidentally played acoustic guitar on David Bowie's *Space Oddity* album, told me his recollections of that seminal weekend.

"My memories of the festival are that it was very small and very rudimentary but a lot of fun. The weather was quite nice that day but a bit cold and I played on the only stage, 'scaffolding and tarps' in the afternoon. I remember thinking what a lovely spot it was and apart from the sound of the music it was very quiet and very peaceful. I had to go off and do another gig in the evening so unfortunately I wasn't able to stay and see Marc Bolan. Michael Eavis was a real gentleman on the day and over the ten years that followed I played the festival many times, sometimes just turning up and asking for a spot, which I always got! Nobody had any idea on that day what it would become but when I dropped in to visit the following year it had already grown massively and the foundations of the larger event were already apparent. They were great times, very relaxed and informal and the first festival was a great start to a great event."

Andrew Kerr in his memoirs wrote, "I am pleased that the formula evolved for holding an event of this type and that it did not end up a disaster, those I have met since can only say that they loved it, or made remarks like, it's a legend."

The last word should go to Michael, who in his foreword reveals, "The festival has now grown beyond my wildest dreams."

Mick Jagger's appearance on the Pyramid stage
was perhaps the most eagerly awaited of all time.

Index